Walk Tall, You're a Daughter of God

Walk Tall, You're a Daughter of God

JAMIE GLENN

DESERET BOOK COMPANY
SALT LAKE CITY, UTAH

Library of Congress Cataloging-in-Publication Data

Glenn, Jamie, 1953–
    Walk Tall, you're a daughter of God / Jamie Glenn.
      p.   cm.
    Includes bibliographical references and index.
    ISBN 0-87579-868-3
    1. Christian life—Mormon authors—Juvenile literature. 2. Women
in the Mormon Church—Juvenile literature. [1. Mormons.
2. Christian life.] I. Title. II. Title: Walk tall, you are a
daughter of God.
BX8656.G54   1994
248.8'33—dc20   94-3696
                                                                  CIP
                                                                  AC

Printed in the United States of America

10 9 8 7 6 5 4 3 2 1

Right now I have a prayer deep within my heart,
A prayer for each of you there is a special part—
That you remember who you are and him who
 lives above.
Please seek for him and live his way;
You'll feel his love.

Long before the time you can remember,
Our Father held you in his arms so tender.
Those loving arms released you as he sent you
 down to earth.
He said, "My child, I love you.
Don't forget your great worth."

This life on earth we knew would not be easy.
At times we lose our way; his path we may not see.
But remember always that you are not alone.
He'll take your hand. He loves you!
He will guide you home.

(Chorus)
Walk tall, you're a daughter, a child of God.
Be strong and remember who you are.
Try to understand, you're part of his great plan.
He's closer than you know.
Reach up; he'll take your hand.

CONTENTS

CHAPTER ONE

Walk Tall,
You're a Daughter of God

I do not consider myself to be a musician, and I know very little about music theory. I play two songs on the piano, "Sweet Hour of Prayer" (slowly) and "Silent Night" (in season). I am one of the grown-ups who remembers well my mother saying, "Jamie, you'll be sorry when you grow up if you don't practice the piano now." I admit it—I'm sorry! My family has always had fun with music in our home. We enjoyed singing together. I have sisters who *did* practice the piano and play well, and my brother and sisters and I all play a little on the guitar.

I had written several songs using my guitar, just to express things I was feeling. My sisters and I sang one or two when requested by my mother for stake Mutual meetings, and my brother and his friends made several sound better than I could, but mostly they were just sung in my room.

I had been out of college several years when I was called to teach the Beehives in my ward. At that time I was working full-time on Temple Square with Wednesday as

1

my day off. This was back before the consolidated Sunday meeting schedule, when Mutual was held on Wednesday evenings and the Young Women lessons were not taught on Sunday. I spent most Wednesdays preparing Mutual lessons for my girls.

One Tuesday night I received a phone call from a friend who knew I didn't work on Wednesdays. He asked if I wanted to spend the next day hiking in the mountains above Lindon, Utah. I said yes, knowing that sometime before Wednesday night I would need to prepare a Mutual lesson. Wednesday was a great day for hiking—perfectly clear and comfortably warm. It was a good day to be out in the beautiful world. I thought about my girls that day and had strong feelings that there was a message I needed to give them that night.

I arrived home about five o'clock that evening and hurried downstairs to prepare my lesson. Soon the lesson was prepared, and the song "Walk Tall, You're a Daughter of God" was written. The melody came first as I put together some guitar chords that sounded good together, and part of the tune for the chorus was borrowed from a song I had written for my mom for Mother's Day. The words came quickly, with only a few changes. I drew small circles with arrows between them on a piece of lined paper so I could remember when the melody went up and down. Then I quickly typed the words to the new song so I could give a copy to my girls at Mutual. I took my guitar with me to the church and was on time for prayer meeting at seven. When I sang the song as part of my lesson, I said to the girls, "I hope I remember how this goes." I did remember how it went, and I think they needed the message.

I am grateful that Heavenly Father blessed me in writing this song for those girls. I have a hard time saying, "Then I went down to my room and *I* wrote the song." I know I couldn't and didn't do it by myself. I remember the feelings I had more than I remember actually writing the song. I believe the Lord when he says, "Behold, I will tell you in your mind and in your heart, by the Holy Ghost, which shall come upon you and which shall dwell in your heart." (D&C 8:2.)

I have realized that the message to "Walk Tall, You're a Daughter of God" is universal. It applies to all of us, no matter what our stage is in life. It was written for young women, but I need the message too. My little nieces all have T-shirts or sweatshirts with the words "Walk Tall" ironed on the shirts as a reminder. I was touched by the truth of the words as my sisters and I sang the song at my grandmother's funeral: "He's closer than you know. Reach up; he'll take your hand." I know the message of this song is true, and I believe it is a message from our Heavenly Father.

Some years ago, a member of the stake high council spoke in my ward's sacrament meeting. The things he said in his talk have helped me refocus my life many times. He said over and over as he spoke, "What *if* the Plan is true?" He spoke about the Plan of Salvation and about how we should be living our lives *if* the Plan is true. We know what the Plan is: that each of us has lived with Heavenly Father, that he knows us and is close to us now that we have come to earth to learn and be tested, and that one day we will return to him. That is a brief summary of the Plan. We know there are many more wonderful details, including the fact that we have a Savior who, through his atonement, makes the completion of the whole Plan possible.

No matter how much knowledge we have of the Plan, or even if we wonder if there is a Plan, we can still ask ourselves, "What *if* the Plan is true?" And what if it is? If it is true that we have lived with Heavenly Father, that he knows us now, and that we are going to return to him—then there is purpose to our lives! If the Plan is true, then there is more to life than just this very day, and it is worth everything for us to learn about and follow the Plan. "Try to understand, you're part of his great Plan!" ("Walk Tall, You're a Daughter of God.")

The Young Women Theme is a great statement of belief that is known by thousands of young women throughout the world. Every Sunday, and often midweek, this theme is repeated from memory in many languages by young women and their leaders. What *if* the first line of the Young Women Theme is true? "We are daughters of our Heavenly Father who loves us, and we love Him." If it is true, then this gives great meaning to our lives. As a Young Women leader, I memorized the theme, and I know it in my mind. Some of the time I know it in my heart—and that is when it makes a difference.

It is not enough to know about the Plan in our minds, where we intellectually think, "Sure, I am a child of God." We need to move this knowledge from our minds into our hearts, where it makes a difference in our lives, gives direction for everything we do, and provides a sure foundation for every decision we make.

I appreciate an important dimension of learning taught by Elder Boyd K. Packer: "We become so accustomed to learning through our physical senses—by sight and sound and smell, by taste and touch—that some of us seem to learn in no other way. "But there are spiritual things that are not registered that way at all. Some things we simply feel, not as we feel something we touch, but as we feel something we *feel*. There are things, spiritual things, that are registered in our minds and recorded in our memories as pure knowledge." (*Ensign,* May 1977, p. 54.) As we understand in our minds and in our hearts that we are daughters of God and that there is a gospel plan, we are drawing upon those memories, for we have lived with him and have known him and his plan perfectly.

The feelings Elder Packer speaks of are the feelings we have when we learn through the Spirit. We are told in Romans, "The Spirit itself beareth witness with our spirit, that we are the children of God." (Romans 8:16.) Only through the Spirit can we know we are children of God. Learning through study and observation *and* our feelings, through the witness of the Spirit, is a real way to learn—the only way to learn the things of Heavenly Father.

Four-year-old Abby approached her mother one day with a sincere question: "Mom, shouldn't we be packing or something?"

Her mother responded with her own question: "Packing for what, Abby?"

Abby explained, "You know, for when we go back to heaven to live with Heavenly Father."

Her mother wisely took time to teach Abby that the only things we get to take with us when we go back to live with Heavenly Father are the things we have learned and our families. Abby had so hoped to take her blanket and some paper with her. She loves to draw. Knowing that heaven will be a wonderful place, she suggested that there might be a whole room full of paper or even paper in every room "so kids can draw anytime they want."

Abby's question, "Shouldn't we be packing or something?" is really a very good question. The answer is "Yes, we should be packing"—maybe not packing our bags, but packing into our lives all those things that will make our journey here rich and full, and packing into our minds those things that are of most importance and will bring us the greatest happiness: knowledge about who we really are, about the purpose of this life, and of our Heavenly Father's plan. We should be accumulating experiences that will allow us to return to him, storing up all that he is so willing to give, keeping our covenants, helping others enjoy their journey, and preparing for the time when we will be with him again. Abby is right—we should be packing.

We read in the Book of Mormon about Lehi's vision of the tree of life. He learned through this vision many wonderful things about the Plan. He shared his sacred experience with his four sons, telling them what he had seen and how he felt about it. One of his sons, Nephi, "was desirous also that [he] might see, and hear, and know of these things, by the power of the Holy Ghost." (1 Nephi 10:17.) He wanted to see for himself and hear for himself and know for himself the things that his father had witnessed. He had faith, "believing that the Lord was able to make them known unto [him]" (1 Nephi 11:1), and he was blessed to see the vision and know for himself. The Lord will make known to each of us, as he made known to Nephi, that the Plan is true and that we each have a part in it. We must desire to know, ask to know, and believe that the Lord is able to make it known—and he will.

Not long ago, a bishop called a young man into his office to discuss whether or not this young man would serve a mission. The young man told the bishop he had decided he was not going on a mission; he had no feelings that the Church was true and had no desire to serve. The bishop told the prospective missionary that, of course, the choice was his to make, but he wisely challenged him to live for two weeks as if he *were* preparing to serve a mission. The bishop read to the young man from Alma 32, where we are told that we can "experiment upon the word." (V. 27.) He challenged the young man to experiment and test the word of the Lord by living as if he knew the gospel was true, by praying often, reading the scriptures, and obeying every commandment—just in case it was true.

The young man accepted the challenge, at first only to prove that the experiment would produce no results. However, at the end of the two weeks he returned to the bishop's office wearing a white shirt, with his hair trimmed above the ears, and with a sweet testimony in his heart that he desired to serve the Lord, whom he recognized and loved.

We too can experiment upon the Lord's words and see if living as if we know the Plan is true doesn't create in us a belief that it is. Alma's counsel continues: "Even if ye can no more than desire to believe, let this desire work in you, even until ye believe in a manner that ye can give place for a portion of my words." (Alma 32:27.) Often the beginning of knowing that the Plan is true is *desiring* to know if it is true. We can let this desire work in us *and* experiment upon the Lord's words. As we continue to make efforts, nourish our understanding, and live as if the Plan is true, our faith will be increased, and it will surely "enlarge [our] soul," "enlighten [our] understanding," and "be delicious" to us. (Alma 32:28.)

Elder Merlin R. Lybbert told the story of an enterprising turkey who gathered his flock together and, with instructions and demonstrations, taught them all how to fly. "All afternoon they enjoyed soaring and flying and the thrill of seeing new vistas. After the meeting, all of the turkeys walked home." (*Ensign,* May 1990, p. 82.) They had learned something wonderful that would allow them to rise above where they had always been, that would give them a broader vision of life and of where they fit into the world. The turkeys did nothing with that valuable, newfound knowledge. Instead, they remained on the ground to do what turkeys do, and they missed out on a richer and fuller life.

The vision we have of life will depend upon what we do with our knowledge of the Plan. If we know and apply our knowledge that there is a plan, that we have a Heavenly Father who loves us, and that we are a part of his plan, we *can* enjoy soaring and flying and the thrill of seeing new vistas. We were not meant to walk home with our eyes on the ground but to walk tall, having a rich and full vision of the purpose of our lives.

With this knowledge, we have the vision that Helen Keller spoke of when, late in her life, a reporter asked her what could be worse than being blind. She responded: "Having eyes to see . . . and no vision." (Quoted in Lloyd D. Newell, "Music and the Spoken Word," February 2, 1992.) We are blessed not only to have the eyes to see but also a clear vision of purpose and perspective in our lives. We are blessed to know "[we're] part of his great plan."

Chapter Two

Walk Tall

I was the nursery leader in my ward. I had not been serving long when one Sunday in sacrament meeting I sat a few rows behind James and his family. James was two years old and one of my favorite class members. Partway through sacrament meeting, James was kneeling next to his mother, facing backward, with his chin resting on his hands. He was watching the activity of several small children sitting on the row behind him. James was being quiet and sitting relatively still in this position when he looked up and caught my eyes, and he realized I was smiling at him. James looked surprised. Then he smiled broadly and shook his mother's shoulder to get her attention. From three rows back, I heard him announce to his mother, "Mommy, Mommy! Look! There's . . . There's . . . There's . . . Somebody!" He didn't know my name in that excited moment, but he knew I was Somebody.

I am Somebody and you are Somebody. Wouldn't it be great if every morning we could get up and look in the mirror and say with real feeling and excitement, "Now, there's Somebody!" It is okay to feel that way about ourselves. It would please Heavenly Father greatly for each of us to feel excited to be who we are. We could all do a lot more to help his kingdom *and* we would be a lot happier if we all had good feelings like that. He wants us to know that we are Somebody.

It is normal for three-year-old Megan and her mother to tell each other "I love you." One day Megan's mother said, "I sure love you, Megan."

Megan began with her usual reply, "I love you too, Mommy." Then, with a new twist to the usual but sincere conversation, Megan said, "And I love myself too. Do you love yourself, Mom?"

Megan's mother was surprised by this but answered, "I do, Megan. Why do you love yourself?"

Megan responded, "Because I am sweet and happy and I am good at gymnastics!"

We each have good qualities and good abilities. It is okay to recognize them. In fact, it is part of knowing who we are to recognize, develop, and love the good things about ourselves. It is important for us to recognize our good qualities, such being sweet and happy. And it is good to recognize our abilities, like being good at gymnastics. I hope we can each say, like Megan, "And I love myself too."

When the Lord said, "I will make a man more precious than fine gold" (Isaiah 13:12), do we think, "He meant everyone but me"? What if the Plan is true? What if we have lived with Heavenly Father, and what if he knows us now? What if there is purpose to this life and each of us will return to him? Then each of our lives is "more precious than fine gold," and our worth is great to Heavenly Father.

This could be a very short chapter as we talk about why we can "walk tall," because the *why* is very basic and simple. It is so simple but sometimes hard to comprehend: We can walk tall simply because we are daughters of God. If we do not walk tall, it is probably because we are believing things that are not true about who we really are or we are not looking to the true source of our worth. We spend a lot of time looking in the world to find our worth, but we will not find it there. It is within us, simply because we are daughters of God. There is nothing in the world that can add to our worth—not money, not possessions, not clothes, not titles, not other people. Our worth is not of this world.

We often use the terms *self-worth, self-image,* and *self-esteem* interchangeably. These terms are related to each other, but we need to understand how they are different from each other. Two of the three may change, but only one of them is sure to be constant. Self-worth is our real value—who we really are. It does not change. It doesn't need to because it cannot get better than it already is. It is 100 percent prime! We are 100 percent prime! Absolutely the best! Why? Because we are daughters of God.

Our self-image is how we view ourselves. This can change a lot in each of our lives. On good days we see ourselves in a positive way, so we have a good self-image. On bad days we see ourselves in a negative light, and our image of ourselves may change drastically in a negative way.

Self-esteem is how we feel about ourselves. This varies right along with our self-image. If our self-image is negative, our self-esteem will be low. If our self-image is positive, we will esteem ourselves more highly and will feel good about being who we are. We need to see ourselves in such a way that our self-image matches our self-worth. Then our self-esteem will be high, and we will feel good about being who we are.

President Ezra Taft Benson gave us great and simple counsel when he said, "A wholesome view of self-worth . . . is best established by a close relationship with God." (*Ensign*, May 1986, p. 6.) Since God is the source of our worth, it is to him that we turn to understand that worth.

I have a friend who was born near the end of February, so her astrological sign is Pisces. One day she read some information about the supposed characteristics of a Pisces. It went something like this: "As a Pisces you have a tendency to be self-centered. You have little ambition in life and probably count on others to choose your life for you. You often do not stay with a project until it is completed; therefore you may lack dependability." As my friend read this, her expression soured and she commented, "Oh, I guess I am a lot like that. I thought I was pretty dependable, but I guess not. And maybe I don't really have much ambition." She was negatively affected because she believed what she had read. She viewed herself (self-image) in a negative way, so her self-esteem dropped drastically, and her self-worth was forgotten.

The next day my friend was more positive and much more like herself. She commented, "You know, for a while I believed what I read yesterday. But I went home and read my patriarchal blessing, and now I know who I am." She went to the Source, to the one who knows her the best and loves her the most. Her self-worth became clear, her self-image matched that worth, and her self-esteem was as Heavenly Father intended.

I love Sister Elaine L. Jack's statement about our patriarchal blessings. "Have you ever heard of one which says, 'I am sorry—You're a loser. Do the best you can on earth, and we'll see you in about seventy years.'" (*Ensign,* November 1989, p. 87.) That is not the way Heavenly Father sees any of us. I am sure in each of our blessings there are sweet expressions of Heavenly Father's love for us, reminders of the close relationship we had with him before coming to this earth, and great promises of our potential and eternal possibilities. We can believe what our patriarchal blessings tell us about who we really are. We should read our patriarchal blessings—not our horoscopes—to know ourselves better and to receive direction in our lives.

What a blessing it is to know and feel the great love Heavenly Father has for his children. What a difference it makes in being able to walk tall when we feel that love in our lives. "The love of the Father is not limited to those who worship and obey him, although their rewards will be greatest, but it is extended to all of his children. The Father's work, and his glory, is to love and to lift all of his children as far as they will allow him. Latter-day Saints believe it is the intention of the Father to make all human beings as happy as they possibly can be." (*Encyclopedia of Mormonism,* edited by Daniel H. Ludlow [New York: Macmillan, 1992], 2:549.) He wants each of us to be as happy as we possibly can be. We need to allow him to "love and to lift" us by recognizing him and his great love for us. When we feel his love, we feel happy; these blessings go very much together.

Two-year-old Bradley knows that Heavenly Father loves him. He isn't old enough to read yet, but he often opens up the scriptures, turns to any page, and "reads" out loud, "Heavenly Father loves me." Bradley knows the scriptures are full of teachings about Heavenly Father's love, and he reminds his family of that every time he "reads" the scriptures.

The scriptures explain beautifully that "the love of God . . . is the most desirable above all things. . . . Yea, and the most joyous to the soul." (1 Nephi 11:22–23.) We also read Paul's teaching that "neither death, nor life, nor angels, nor principalities, nor powers, nor things present, nor things to come, nor height, nor depth, nor any other creature, shall be able to separate us from the love of God." (Romans 8:39.) As our Eternal Father, God's capacity to love is beyond our understanding. His personal love for each of us is greater than we can comprehend, but we can feel it fully and know that it is "the most desirable above all things." No matter what else we find desirable here on earth, it cannot compare to the feeling of his perfect, personal, and unconditional love.

When I was twelve, I needed to know that Heavenly Father loved me, that my worth was within me and didn't come from the kind of socks I wore. That may not sound like a major trauma, but it was to me. My family had lived in California since I was four years old. The summer I was twelve, my Dad was transferred back to Utah. We moved into our house in August just a few weeks before I would begin eighth grade. I had met the girls my age at church, but I had not had a lot of interaction with them and had not yet gotten in with a group or found a good friend.

I remember nervously walking to the bus stop the first day of school. This was in the "olden days" before girls wore pants to school, so my outfit was a new plaid skirt and sweater bought especially for the first day. I was feeling self-conscious. I was the "new girl." I was unsure of myself and didn't particularly want to be noticed. As I approached the group of junior high school students, it seemed that all of their eyes moved to my feet, and they stayed there—staring. It didn't take me long to realize why. I looked at all of the other girls' feet. They all wore thin socks rolled down over their ankles—not folded down, but rolled. My socks were thick and were not rolled or even folded down but stretched halfway up my calves— the way we wore them in California. I wanted to be in California right then, where everyone wore socks like mine.

I don't remember how long it was until I got new socks. But I do remember feeling different, like I was not a part of the group, and feeling looked down upon because of my thick socks stretched halfway up my calves. My image of myself because of that incident was negative, and I let myself feel stupid. I remember someone telling me during that time, "Jamie, no one can make you feel inferior without your consent." I guess I had given my consent. I thought that different socks meant I didn't have as much worth as the others. I know now that it really didn't change my worth when I changed my socks. After a short while I became involved with those girls in church and school activities and made some wonderful friends. And they probably don't even remember what kind of socks I wore the first day of school when I was in the eighth grade.

It is sometimes easier for us to believe that everyone's life has worth except our own. We know our own weaknesses so well, and we compare our weaknesses with others' strengths. Heavenly Father doesn't compare us to anyone else. Who we are is who he wants to come to him. Who we are is who he loves. If we doubt our worth, we are doubting his ability and his creations.

We can ask him if it is true that we are his daughters, if we really have worth, and if we are Somebody. We can ask him if he knows us and if he loves us. He will bless us each to know, "for every one that asketh receiveth." (Matthew 7:8.) We can feel of his love, "which passeth knowledge" (Ephesians 3:19) and is "most desirable above all things" (1 Nephi 11:22). And we can walk tall because we know that we are daughters of God.

CHAPTER THREE

You're a Daughter of God

To really walk tall we must first understand that we are each a daughter of God. In order to know *who* we are, we must first know *whose* we are. Without an understanding of our relationship with Heavenly Father, our vision of ourselves will not be accurate, and we may look at ourselves through the eyes of the world instead of seeing "things as they really are." (Jacob 4:13.) President Marion G. Romney put this understanding in perspective: "That man is a child of God is the most important knowledge available to mortals." (*Ensign,* July 1973, p. 14.)

Remember, the first part of the Plan is that we have lived with Heavenly Father. It is true that "long before the time you can remember, our Father held you in his arms so tender." ("Walk Tall, You're a Daughter of God.") I have heard it said that we have a great, sure knowledge of God our Heavenly Father, but it is locked up within us right now. Brigham Young said it this way: "I want to tell you, each and every one of you, that you are well acquainted with God our Heavenly Father. . . . You are all well acquainted with him, for there is not a soul of you but what has lived in his house and dwelt with him year after year." (*Discourses of Brigham Young,* compiled by John A. Widtsoe [Salt Lake City: Deseret Book Co., 1975], p. 50.) Surely our trying to find him now is trying to remember what we have known so well.

I also love this statement by President Ezra Taft Benson: "Nothing is going to startle us more when we pass through the veil to the other side than to realize how well we know our Father and how familiar his face is to us." ("Jesus Christ—Gifts and Expectations," *Speeches of the Year: BYU Devotional and Ten-Stake Fireside Addresses, 1974* [Provo, Utah: BYU Press, 1975], p. 313.) We have been with him and been close to him. We have known him well, and he has known and does know us well. It would be wonderful to see just for a brief moment what we knew before we came to this earth. Instead, we walk by faith, learn about him, and let our feelings tell us that we do know him and that he knows us.

Several years ago I went to Disneyland with my sisters and a friend. The crowds were large and the lines were long. I couldn't remember ever seeing so many people in one place before. After a long day of playing hard, I sat on the curb of Main Street waiting for a parade to begin. I watched thousands of people, some old and many young, some speaking English and many who were not, some looking happy and many looking lost. The thought came into my mind, "I wonder how many of these people know that they are children of God?" I knew that they all were, whether they knew it or not. I felt overwhelmed by the reality that God is the Father of us all—not just those who happened to be at Disneyland that day but everyone who has ever lived or will ever live upon the earth.

I feel gratitude as I realize what a blessing it is to know that he is my Father. It saddens me that not everyone remembers him, and I feel the responsibility to help others understand their heritage. We are so blessed to know not only that he is our Father but also that he is very aware of us and can be personally involved in our lives.

My sister Julie and her husband, Dan, were expecting their second child when they moved one August from Salt Lake City to Salem, Oregon, where Dan would attend law school. Annie, their first child, had turned two years old in July. Because their families and their doctor were in Salt Lake City, Julie and Dan decided that she would return there to have the baby. The baby was due the first week in November, so Julie and Annie flew home to stay with my parents the first part of October. It was planned that Dan would fly into Salt Lake City around the 28th of October, the doctor would induce labor the next day, and their little family would all be together for this important occasion. I know that many babies are born each day, but this was a really big thing because it was *my* family. This was a very important event!

About ten o'clock at night on October 18, I received a telephone call from my sister Tracy. She announced, "Jamie, Mom and Dad have taken Julie to the hospital. She is in labor!" My first thought was, "I hope her labor lasts for ten days so Dan will be here." Of course, Dan had already been telephoned. He had made arrangements to be on the next flight from Portland to Salt Lake, but the flight wasn't until the next morning. I told Tracy to have

Dad call me no matter what time the baby was born—after all, I was the child's aunt!

I didn't sleep in my bed that night. In fact, I didn't sleep much at all. I covered myself up with a blanket on the floor by the telephone. I lay there wide awake for several hours thinking about what was happening. I was basking in the feeling that there is a Plan, that there was a spirit so recently with Heavenly Father who was going to be a part of my family. It was also very clear to me that I had been with Heavenly Father, that there is purpose in this life, and that there is more to life than just this very minute.

When the telephone rang about two in the morning, I picked up the receiver partway through the first ring. It was my dad. "It's a girl! Jennifer is here, and she is beautiful. Everything went well. Hold on—here comes your mom with the baby now." Dad held the telephone up to Mom's ear as she walked by holding the brand new bundle. "I'm on my way to give Jennifer her first bath. She has a lot of hair and is really beautiful!" Because Dan could not arrive until morning, my mom got to be there for the delivery—a sweet experience for a mom and grandma to have!

Dad and I congratulated each other (as if we really had anything to do with it), and I lay back down on the floor, again experiencing a glimpse of what it feels like to *know* for sure that Heavenly Father lives. I knew that Jennifer had been with him recently, and I knew that I was his daughter in that same way.

The title "child of God" has marvelous meaning, carries tremendous honor, and gives us great privileges—much more so than worldly titles. Somehow "cheerleader," "president," and "homecoming queen" mean less when we recognize that these titles are temporary and really have nothing to do with our worth as a person. It is because we are children of God that we have great worth when we come to this earth. This title belongs to each of us, even if we are not aware of it or don't recognize it or believe it. In the October 1992 general conference, Elder Neal A. Maxwell said, "As we come to know to Whom we belong, the other forms of belonging cease to mean very much." (*Ensign,* November 1992, p. 66.) How true that is, and how blessed we are to know it.

I love to reflect on a wonderful experience Moses had as he learned that he was a son of God. We read in Moses chapter 1 that Moses "saw God face to face, and he talked with him." (V. 2.) Moses learned about God and his great works, and he even "beheld the world upon which he was created; . . . and all the children of men which are, and which were created." (V. 8.) As God talked with Moses, he told Moses several times that Moses was his son. In verse 4 He said, "Behold, *thou art my son.*" (Emphasis added.) In verse 6 he said, "I have a work for thee, Moses, *my son.*" (Emphasis added.) Then in verse 7 he said, "Behold, this one thing I show unto thee, *Moses, my son.*" (Emphasis added.) I think those words would have a powerful impact on me if Heavenly Father told me himself that I was his daughter. This had an impact on Moses. As we read on, we learn that "the presence of God withdrew from Moses, . . . and Moses was left unto himself." (V. 9.)

Then something happened to Moses that sometimes happens to us after we have had a powerful spiritual experience. "Satan came tempting him, saying: Moses, *son of man,* worship me." (V. 12; emphasis added.) By calling

Moses "son of man," I think Satan was saying to him, "You're really not a son of God; you're really not someone of worth." Moses' response shows that knowing he was a son of God enabled him to withstand Satan. Verse 13 says, "Moses looked upon Satan and said: Who art thou? *For behold, I am a son of God,* in the similitude of his Only Begotten; and where is thy glory, that I should worship thee?" (Emphasis added.)

Satan may come tempting us, and we need to be able to say, "Who art thou? For behold, *I am a daughter of God!*" That knowledge can give us great strength and enable us to withstand Satan and anyone who tries to tempt us to follow Satan's ways.

Elder Marvin J. Ashton spoke of Satan's evil desire for us to forget that we are children of God: "If he could have his way, Satan would distract us from our heritage. He would have us become involved in a million and one things in this life—probably none of which are very important in the long run—to keep us from concentrating on the things that are really important, particularly the reality that we are God's children. . . . He'd like to keep us so busy with comparatively insignificant things that we don't have time to make the effort to understand where we came from, whose children we are, and how glorious our ultimate homecoming can be!" (*Ensign,* November 1992, p. 22.) We foil Satan's plans when we remember that we have a great heritage and that we are daughters of God. And it is part of Heavenly Father's plan for us that we remember *whose* children we are.

A fable is told about an eagle who thought he was a chicken. When the eagle was very small, he fell from the safety of his nest. A chicken farmer found the eagle, brought him to the farm, and raised him in a chicken coop among his many chickens. The eagle grew up doing what chickens do, living like a chicken, and believing he was a chicken.

A naturalist came to the chicken farm to see if what he had heard about an eagle acting like a chicken was really true. He knew that an eagle is king of the sky. He was surprised to see the eagle strutting around the chicken coop, pecking at the ground, and acting very much like a chicken. The farmer explained to the naturalist that this bird was no longer an eagle. He was now a chicken because he had been trained to be a chicken and he believed that he was a chicken.

The naturalist knew there was more to this great bird than his actions showed as he "pretended" to be a chicken. He was born an eagle and had the heart of an eagle, and nothing could change that. The man lifted the eagle onto the fence surrounding the chicken coop and said, "Eagle, thou art an eagle. Stretch forth thy wings and fly." The eagle moved slightly, only to look at the man; then he glanced down at his home among the chickens in the chicken coop where he was comfortable. He jumped off the fence and continued doing what chickens do. The farmer was satisfied. "I told you it was a chicken," he said.

The naturalist returned the next day and tried again to convince the farmer and the eagle that the eagle was born for something greater. He took the eagle to the top of the farmhouse and spoke to him: "Eagle, thou art an eagle. Thou dost belong to the sky and not to the earth. Stretch forth thy wings and fly." The large bird looked at the man, then again down into the chicken coop. He jumped from the man's arm onto the roof of the farm-house.

Knowing what eagles are really all about, the naturalist asked the farmer to let him try one more time. He would return the next day and prove that this bird was an eagle. The farmer, convinced otherwise, said, "It is a chicken."

The naturalist returned the next morning to the chicken farm and took the eagle and the farmer some distance away to the foot of a high mountain. They could not see the farm nor the chicken coop from this new setting. The man held the eagle on his arm and pointed high into the sky where the bright sun was beckoning above. He spoke: "Eagle, thou art an eagle! Thou dost belong to the sky and not to the earth. Stretch forth thy wings and fly." This time the eagle stared skyward into the bright sun, straightened his large body, and stretched his massive wings. His wings moved, slowly at first, then surely and powerfully. With the mighty screech of an eagle, he flew. (In Sterling Grant Ellsworth, *To Know Me Is to Love Me* [Eugene, Oregon: Sterling G. Ellsworth, 1982), pp. 151–52.)

We were born to be eagles. Because of our beginning and the fact that we are daughters of God, we have great potential, not just to strut around the ground and merely exist in this life, but to reach the highest heights and see the greatest vistas. The eagle needed to remember that he was an eagle. That fact would not change, even if he thought otherwise. We need to remember that we are daughters of God. That wonderful fact will never change, even if we have believed otherwise. Because of this truth, we have the power and potential to rise high and be who we were meant to be.

President Gordon B. Hinckley told the young women of the Church, "You will not need to be reminded to be virtuous, you will not need to be reminded to be clean, if you will remember always that you are a daughter of God, that a portion of his divinity is within you, and that you must make an accounting to him." (*The Wonderful Thing That Is You and the Wonderful Good You Can Do* [Salt Lake City: The Church of Jesus Christ of Latter-day Saints, 1986], p. 7.) This knowledge is a basis for other knowledge and a foundation for understanding who we are and living the way we should be living. If we really remember this in our minds and in our hearts, obedience and happiness will follow in a natural course.

The ancient apostle Paul spoke to the Athenians about "the unknown God" whom they "ignorantly worshipped." After hearing from Paul, some did not believe his words, and some wanted to know more. His declaration to them included counsel that "they should seek the Lord, if they are willing to find him, for he is not far from every one of us." (Acts 17:27, JST.) I hope we are "willing to find him, for he is not far from every one of us," and we do not need to be very far from him. Please "remember always that you are not alone. He'll take your hand—He loves you! He will guide you home." ("Walk Tall, You're a Daughter of God.")

CHAPTER FOUR

He Is Aware of You

I had a wonderful opportunity one summer to go with a tour group to Israel and then to the Passion Play in Oberammergau, Germany. At the end of the trip we flew from Zurich, Switzerland, to New York and then home to Salt Lake City. Our flight from Zurich to New York was on a large, double-decker airplane. We had been flying over the Atlantic Ocean for several hours, dinner had been served and eaten, and the movie was over. Our tour group occupied most of the seats on the top level of the airplane, with a dozen or so people who were not with our group filling in the rest of the upstairs seats. In Zurich it was almost time for bed, so we were feeling sleepy. Most of the shades were drawn over the windows even though it was light outside, and it was quiet except for the sounds of the flight attendants moving around in the back room. I had dozed off and was sleeping as soundly as it is possible to sleep on an airplane.

I woke up suddenly as a woman yelled, "Help! Help! Is there a doctor on the plane?" A young mother was hurrying down the aisle, holding a limp baby in her arms.

The baby appeared lifeless, and the mother was frantic. The flight attendants were not trained for anything like this. The passengers were concerned, and we all felt helpless. And remember, we were over the middle of the Atlantic Ocean—probably halfway to anywhere.

The urgent request for a doctor spread quickly, and a young man ran up the stairs from the lower level of the plane to the weeping mother. The mother stood helplessly and hopefully hugging her baby. The feelings I had while watching this were dramatic. I was praying in my heart that this baby would be okay. I knew I would want the plane to turn around and go back if we could get help sooner by doing so. Never in my life had I felt such united concern for one person before. No one on the plane was sleeping anymore.

I wasn't sure what was going on behind the drawn curtain in the back, but a short while later we heard the baby whimper, and in another few moments the baby cried. Sometimes hearing a baby cry on an airplane can be an irritation, but not this time. The prayer in my heart was now a prayer of thanks. The baby had had a very high fever and had gone into convulsions. The young doctor was able to give her an injection of a medication he happened to have with him. With this, and by cooling off her tiny, feverish body, the convulsions stopped and the fever lowered.

I was grateful this story ended the way it did. I learned that each life is important. Everyone on that airplane would have done anything to help that baby, and everyone's heart was hurting for that distraught mother. I learned that sometimes we are powerless and must depend upon our Heavenly Father to help us when what we need is beyond our power. I also felt that even though we were far away from anywhere, we were not far away from him. He knew we were on that airplane, and he knew the need of that little child.

Heavenly Father is aware of us, our every feeling, and our every need even when we feel far away. He could not love us any more, know us any better, or be more aware of us if we were his only child. I am grateful to the author who said, "The sun with all the planets rotating around it can ripen the smallest bunch of grapes as though it had nothing else to do." (As quoted by Vaughn J. Featherstone in *Charity Never Faileth* [Salt Lake City: Deseret Book Co., 1980], p. 79.) Surely Heavenly Father is aware of us and blesses our individual lives "as though [he] had nothing else to do."

Part of the time I was growing up, I shared a bedroom with one of my sisters. As we would go to bed at night, I would either be sure I said my prayers before my sister said hers, or I would wait until she had crawled into bed and then say my prayers. I had a hard time understanding how Heavenly Father could hear me *and* my sister if we were both praying at the same time. I wanted his full attention when I prayed to him. I still don't know *how* he can be aware of us all, hear us all, and know us all at the same time—but I know he can.

Like most three-year-olds, Megan asks a lot of questions. Usually one question leads to three or four more as she asks *how* or *why* after each response, wanting to really understand and know all the details. One day Megan asked a very thoughtful question: "How does Heavenly Father hear us when we think about him?" That's a good question. I don't know *how* he does it, but I know he does.

And I do know *why* he does. It is because he loves us so much, is so aware of each of us, and is so close to us that he even knows when we are thinking about him. I know he can "hear us when we think about him," and I am grateful that Megan knows this too.

In the Book of Mormon we read about what took place in the Americas following the Savior's crucifixion. We are told in 3 Nephi chapter 8 that there were earthquakes, fires, tempests, thunderings, lightnings, and whirlwinds. Some cities were sunk into the depths of the sea, and other cities were covered by mountains. With this great destruction many lives were lost; some people drowned, some were slain by fallen buildings, and some were even "carried away in the whirlwind." (V. 16.) This destruction lasted for three hours. Then a thick darkness came upon all the face of the land. This darkness lasted for three days, "and there could be no light." (V. 21.) There was great mourning among the survivors "because of the darkness and the great destruction which had come upon them." (V. 23.)

The people heard the voice of Jesus Christ telling them that the destruction had taken place because of wickedness. He declared his divinity to the people and invited them to come unto him. Then "their mourning was turned into joy, and their lamentations into the praise and thanksgiving unto the Lord Jesus Christ, their Redeemer." (3 Nephi 10:10.)

I love the marvelous scene described in 3 Nephi chapter 11. We read that many of the people gathered at the temple in the land Bountiful. They were talking with each other about Jesus Christ and about what had taken place. As they were talking, they heard a voice "as if it came out of heaven; . . . and it was not a harsh voice, neither was it a loud voice; nevertheless, and notwithstanding it being a small voice it did pierce them that did hear to the center, insomuch that there was no part of their frame that it did not cause to quake; yea, it did pierce them to the very soul, and did cause their hearts to burn." (V. 3.) The people did not understand the voice until it spoke the third time. "And again the third time they did hear the voice, and did open their ears to hear it." (V. 5.)

The voice was the voice of Heavenly Father declaring his Son, Jesus Christ: "Behold my Beloved Son, in whom I am well pleased, in whom I have glorified my name—hear ye him" (V. 7.) Then the people looked up and saw a man descending out of heaven. The Savior stood in their midst and told them, "Behold, I am Jesus Christ, whom the prophets testified shall come into the world." (V. 10.)

The Savior spent time with the people, teaching them many wonderful things, performing miracles, praying with and for them, and blessing the children. But the first thing he did after declaring himself to them was to invite all of them to come forth unto him, to personally feel the prints of the nails in his hands and feet so that they each would know that he was their Savior. And "the multitude went forth, and thrust their hands into his side, and did feel the prints of the nails in his hands and in his feet; and this they did do, going forth *one by one* until they had all gone forth." (V. 15; emphasis added.)

We read that there were twenty-five hundred people in this group—and he had them come forth "one by one." I can't imagine that he hurried the lines of people along, but I think he took time and noticed each individual in a personal way. Why one by one? Because he knew them "one by one" and wanted them each to have a personal experience with him. If the Savior were to come here today, I think he would do the same thing. We are known to him "one by one." He knows each of us and would spend time with each of us and care for us individually. I think he would know each of our circumstances and ask us about them, and we would know that he cares and understands.

How aware are Heavenly Father and Jesus of us, and how well do they know us? Heavenly Father called Joseph Smith by name when He and his Son appeared to Joseph in the Sacred Grove. That was just the beginning of what they knew about Joseph Smith, and our names are only the beginning of what they know about us. We are told that the Lord "knows all the thoughts and intents of the heart; for by his hand were they all created from the beginning." (Alma 18:32.) That's knowing us pretty well.

We also learn in the scriptures that "the Lord searcheth all hearts, and understandeth all the imaginations of the thoughts." (1 Chronicles 28:9.) This means that Heavenly Father knows more than just the outward things we do. He knows our innermost hearts because he "searcheth" our hearts. He understands what is behind the thoughts we have and why we think the way we think, even "all the imaginations of the thoughts." I don't know myself that well. I love this true and simple statement by Elder Neal A. Maxwell: "He knows you better than you know yourself." (*New Era,* January–February 1985, p. 6.)

Megan asked, "How can Heavenly Father hear us when we think about him?" It really goes even beyond that. Heavenly Father is aware of us even when we are not thinking of him. I have a friend whose parents were both killed in an airplane crash several years ago. She is the youngest of nine children and at that time was the only one who was not married. She was left very much alone in this situation. Family members were cleaning out the family home some time after the accident. As one of the sons was going through some papers on his father's desk, he found a note in his father's handwriting. The note simply said, "Rela—Things to Consider," with a list of ten or so items he wanted his daughter to think about. One day before the accident, when Rela was not even aware of it, her father was thinking about her with a special awareness of her needs, desiring to give her counsel for her life ahead. Our Heavenly Father is aware of us even at times when we may not be thinking of him, and even at times when we do not think he is aware of us.

Not long after I bought my first car, I left work one evening and was driving through town, heading toward the freeway that would take me home. The thought came to me, "Jamie, maybe you should check the oil." I didn't know anything about checking the oil, so I dismissed the thought. As I got closer to the freeway, the thought came again, "Maybe you'd better check the oil." I told myself I would wait until I got home and then have Dad check it for me, but the thought came again, and I was convinced that I should check the oil now.

I pulled into a service station, drove into a full-service lane, and unrolled my window. I had heard my dad do this before, so I said, "Check the oil, please." (The attendant had to show me how to unlock the hood so he could lift it up.) He came back to my window a minute later holding a dry dipstick and said, "What oil?" The dipstick was completely dry, without any trace of oil. I have since learned that oil is very important to a car's engine. If I had not stopped, driving the car would have been dangerous, and the engine most likely would have been ruined. I am grateful that Heavenly Father was aware of me and my need—the need I didn't even know I had.

Heavenly Father is aware of the little things and the big things in our lives. He knows how we feel in a very personal way. He is our personal Heavenly Father, and his Son is our personal Savior. Part of the Plan is that a veil has been drawn over our minds, but not over theirs. I think of two-year-old Annie, who felt one day that her mother was not paying enough attention to her. Not demanding but just wondering, Annie asked her mother, "Remember me, Mama?" We do not have to ask Heavenly Father that question. We can be assured that Heavenly Father and his Son do remember each of us very well. They pay great attention to our lives and to our every need.

Life is much more meaningful when this knowledge becomes real to us, when we recognize that the Lord is aware of us personally. He knows us, loves us, and will be close to each of us. He is not just aware of us at the high points in our lives: when we pray to him, when we study the scriptures, when we read our patriarchal blessings, when we go on a mission, or when we get married. He is *always* aware of us.

"Can a woman forget her sucking child, that she should not have compassion on the son of her womb? Yea, they may forget, yet will I not forget thee. Behold, I have graven thee upon the palms of my hands." (Isaiah 49:15–16.) He has personally made a great investment in us. We can be assured that he is always aware of us and will never forget us.

CHAPTER FIVE

Look to the Source

*A*s the children of Israel journeyed in the wilderness, they "spake against God, and against Moses." (Numbers 21:5.) They accused Moses of bringing them out of Egypt to die, and they complained that they didn't like the manna with which they had miraculously been blessed. So "the Lord sent fiery serpents among the people, and they bit the people; and much people of Israel died." (V. 6.) In time, the people recognized their wrongdoing and asked Moses to pray to the Lord that he would take the poisonous serpents from them.

Moses did pray in behalf of the people, and in answer to his prayer the Lord instructed: "Make thee a fiery serpent, and set it upon a pole: and it shall come to pass, that every one that is bitten, when he looketh upon it, shall live." (Numbers 21:8.) Moses did as the Lord instructed, and a way was prepared for the people to be healed. In the Book of Mormon, Nephi taught his people about this experience and told them that not everyone looked, and so not everyone was healed. He explained, "The labor which they had to perform was to look; and because of the simpleness of the way, or the easiness of it, there were many who perished." (1 Nephi 17:41.)

It seems incredible that not everyone would look. It was so simple and straightforward, and the results were sure—if they looked, they would be healed. Alma, another Book of Mormon prophet, explains that they would not look "because they did not believe that it would heal them." (Alma 33:20.) He also sounds surprised that not all would look, as he asks his brethren, "If ye could be healed by merely casting about your eyes that ye might be healed, would ye not behold quickly, or would ye rather harden your hearts in unbelief, and be slothful, that ye would not cast about your eyes, that ye might perish?" (Alma 33:21.)

The children of Israel knew the source to which they needed to turn for healing, but many turned their heads in other directions. Alma also speaks about this concept as he gives commandments to his son Helaman and draws the parallel to our lives. First, he counsels, "Do not let us be slothful because of the easiness of the way." Then he tells us where to look: "The way is prepared, and if we will look we may live forever. . . . Look to God and live." (Alma 37:46–47.)

There is a sure Source in our lives to heal us, no matter what kind of healing we need. The Source is the same for all, even though our lives, situations, and needs are different. The Source is our Heavenly Father. Do we ever look in another direction instead of looking to him? Do we turn our backs and not allow him to help or heal us? Maybe we don't purposely look *away* from him, but are we looking *for* him, and are we living our lives in a manner that will allow us to see him clearly? He is the Source of all we need, and we see everything more clearly by looking to him.

Challenges are a part of our lives—they are part of the Plan. Sometimes when we go through hard times, we get angry with Heavenly Father and blame him. We may deliberately turn away from him and stomp off in another direction, looking for another way to be healed. But there is another option—to recognize that he is the Source, the one who loves us and the only one who can bless us, and it is to him we must turn to find answers and peace. He has prepared a way for us. That way may not always be simple or easy, because difficult things are a part of life. But looking to him as the Source of all we need gives us a simple focus and easy direction for our lives.

A loving invitation to turn to the Source has been extended to each of us: "Come unto me, all ye that labour and are heavy laden, and I will give you rest." (Matthew 11:28.) We have also been invited, "Cast thy burden upon the Lord, and he shall sustain thee." (Psalm 55:22.) He is the Source, the only one who can lift and save and give us peace.

The Savior had challenges too, and he suffered more than we will ever suffer. He wondered if he had been forsaken, but he still turned to the Source of strength and comfort and asked, "My God, my God, why hast thou forsaken me?" (Matthew 27:46.) Elder Neal A. Maxwell explains, "He cried out—not in doubt of his Father's reality, but wondering 'why' at the moment of supreme agony—for Jesus felt so alone. . . . We, too, at times may wonder if we have been forgotten and forsaken. Hopefully, we will do as the Master did and acknowledge that God is still there and never doubt that sublime reality—even though we may wonder and might desire to avoid some of life's experiences." ("But for a Small Moment," *Speeches of the Year: BYU Devotional and Ten-Stake Fireside Addresses, 1974* [Provo, Utah: BYU Press, 1975], p. 445.) There may be times in our lives when we will wonder, "Why?", and that is okay to wonder. We can do as our Savior did, and when we wonder, recognize and ask the Source.

We have probably all felt at times that no one understands us or what we are going through. We may be lucky to have a good friend or family member who can say, "I understand because I have been through something similar in my life." Or we may talk with a professional who says, "I understand because I have studied all about that." But still we wonder if anyone *really* understands. Guess what? There *is* someone who understands in a personal, perfect way, no matter what we feel and no matter what we go through. My favorite scripture of comfort explains this so well: "He shall go forth, suffering pains and afflictions and temptations of every kind; and this that the word might be fulfilled which saith he will take upon him the pains and the sicknesses of his people. And he will take upon him death, that he may loose the bands of death which bind his people; and he will take upon him their *infirmities,* that his bowels may be filled with mercy, according to the flesh, that he may know according to the flesh how to succor his people according to their infirmities." (Alma 7:11–12; emphasis added.)

I have always thought that an infirmity is a disability or physical ailment of some kind. That is part of it. But *infirm* also means "weak of mind, will or character; not solid or stable; of poor or deteriorated vitality; insecure; a foible." (*Webster's Third New International Dictionary,* s.v. "infirm.") So this means that "he will take upon him their [insecurities and personal failings], . . . that he may know according to the flesh how to succor his people according to their [insecurities and personal failings]." He took upon himself our insecurities and personal failings and pains and sicknesses. He took upon himself our weaknesses of mind, will, and character. When we feel that no one understands, he may say, "I do understand—not because I have been through something similar, but because I have been through that very thing for you." And he did it so that he would know exactly how we feel and exactly what we need, so he could help us no matter what we experience.

It is painful to feel lonely, but the Savior took upon himself our pains. That means he understands how we feel when we are the only one of our group of friends who didn't get asked to the homecoming dance. He took upon himself our temptations. That means he understands how hard it can be to say no to temptations when we want to be part of a group. We can feel very insecure when the boy we really like doesn't even know our name. He took upon himself our insecurities so he understands even that. We can see why he is the Source. He is the one who understands! He loves us perfectly and unconditionally, and he has invited each of us to come unto him.

It is up to us to accept his invitation. "Behold, I stand at the door, and knock: if any man hear my voice, and open the door, I will come in to him, and will sup with him, and he with me." (Revelation 3:20.) We must open the door. Although his love is great and his understanding is perfect, and even though he wants to be a part of our lives, it is part of the Plan that he cannot make us turn to him. Because he loves us, he lets us choose. We choose if we will look to him, if we will "open the door" and let him into our lives, and if we will accept his invitation to come unto him.

Alma accepted that invitation. He and his friends had done much to thwart the growth of the Church—and his father was the high priest! When the angel called him to repentance, Alma was "harrowed up by the memory of [his] many sins." (Alma 36:17.) He relates, "I was three days and three nights in the most bitter pain and anguish of soul; and never, until I did cry out unto the Lord Jesus Christ for mercy, did I receive a remission of my sins. But behold, I did cry unto him and I did find peace to my soul." (Alma 38:8.) The relief came only when he turned to the Source.

While traveling in Israel, I had been told that a highlight of my experience would be to get up early and watch the sun rise on the Sea of Galilee. It takes something really important to get me up early, but I decided this was something I wanted to do. I set my alarm for what seemed to be the middle of the night, and then surprisingly easily got out of bed when the alarm rang. Seven or eight of us from our tour group walked the short distance from the kibbutz to the seashore. The world was changing from night black to morning orange, so the promise of a sunrise was sure. I was in the Holy Land, the land the Savior walked and knew and loved. I was standing on the shores of Galilee where he healed and taught and calmed the sea and walked on the water.

We watched reverently as the sun peeked over the hills and then slowly but powerfully rose and reflected perfectly on the sea. I could almost hear the orchestra music, soft, then increasing in volume and power, as the full sun majestically became round above the hills and water. I know the sun rises every day, but I had never before recognized this process or the effect this miracle has on the world. None of us talked out loud. We only whispered as we spoke of the beauty of that scene and of the Light of the World. Because I was where I was, there was a sure correlation between watching a sunrise and knowing that because of it, I could see the day clearly; and knowing that because of the Light of the World I could see life clearly. I could see things "as they really are." (Jacob 4:13.) I thought of C. S. Lewis's great thought, "I believe in Christianity as I believe the Sun has risen, not only because I see it, but because by it I see everything else." (*The Weight of Glory* [New York: Macmillan, 1965], p. 92.) Although we do not see Jesus Christ, we can know he is there and look at life through his light, seeing everything much more clearly. He is the Source and the Light.

We spend a lot of time in our lives looking in many places for what we think we need, and when we don't find it we feel emptier and more unhappy and less peaceful than when we started looking. We make the mistake of looking to the world for things that the world cannot give. We search for peace and happiness in the wrong places, thinking that possessions or other people can give them to us. We may try artificial sources like drugs and alcohol, but they take us in the opposite direction—they are clearly artificial. Where, then, does peace come from? It comes as a gift from the Light of the World: "Peace I leave with you, my peace I give unto you: not as the world giveth, give I unto you." (John 14:27.) He is the Source.

We find peace by finding him: "Acquaint now thyself with him, and be at peace." (Job 22:21.)

My sister Bonnie served a mission in Italy. I remember her telling about an experience she had as she rode on a bus one day and watched a bee buzzing frantically, trying to get out of the bus. From Bonnie's perspective, she could see the opening of the window just above where the bee was buzzing. The bee would get almost to the opening, then turn around and buzz in circles, not seeing far enough ahead to get to where he was trying so hard to go. Bonnie compared this to the perspective our Heavenly Father has as he watches us in our lives. Because he has a broader vision of our lives than we do, he can see what we cannot. He has a clear view of each of us. He knows where we are and where we are going. His love for each of us is great, so we can trust his perspective. We can look to him and seek his guidance in our lives.

In a classic conference talk, President Ezra Taft Benson said, "The proud cannot accept the authority of God giving direction to their lives." (*Ensign*, May 1989, p. 4.) It is not weak to recognize that we need Heavenly Father to direct and guide us. This recognition alone shows strength and wisdom. I love the feeling I have when I read from Proverbs, "A man's heart deviseth his way: but the Lord directeth his steps." (Proverbs 16:9.) What a great team! When our hearts are wise and our desires good, and when we let the Lord direct us, we will go to good places and be where we need to be.

President Benson has also said, "Men and women who turn their lives over to God will find out that He can make a lot more out of their lives than they can. He will deepen their joys, expand their vision, quicken their minds, strengthen their muscles, lift their spirits, multiply their blessings, increase their opportunities, comfort their souls, raise up friends, and pour out peace. Whoever will lose his life to God will find he has eternal life." ("Jesus Christ—Gifts and Expectations," *Speeches of the Year: BYU Devotional and Ten-Stake Fireside Addresses, 1974* [Provo, Utah: BYU Press, 1975], p. 310.) Every part of our lives will be better with him than without him. He can "make a lot more out of [our lives] than we can."

We do not change truth simply by not believing. Truth exists for us to find and embrace, not to change. I love the perspective Elder Graham Doxey gave us when he said, "The questions are not, 'Does God live? Does God love me? Does God speak to me?' The critical question is 'Are you listening to him?'" (*Ensign,* November 1991, p. 25.) Are we listening to him? Are we looking to him and recognizing him as the Source in our lives? We have been promised, "If ye will turn to the Lord with full purpose of heart, and put your trust in him and serve him with all diligence of mind, if ye do this he will, according to his own will and pleasure, deliver you out of bondage." (Mosiah 7:33.) As we "turn to the Lord with full purpose of heart," it is his promise that he will deliver us, for he is the Source.

CHAPTER SIX

"Pray Always, and Be Believing"

*I*t was Independence Day, and I was nine years old. We were living in Sacramento, California. I was the second of five children, and my youngest sister had just been born on June 9. My dad was in Utah, spending several weeks in classes at Brigham Young University with other Church educators as part of his preparation for a new school year. Most summers our whole family enjoyed the time in Utah together, but because we had a brand-new baby it was decided that Dad would go alone this year.

We had just waved good-bye to some cousins who had stopped by on their way through town, and we were walking back into our house when my mom was stung by a bee on one of her big toes. I had remembered Mom telling us about when she was a little girl and was stung by a bee; she had almost died because of a severe allergic reaction. It didn't take long for this allergy to again become obvious. First the toe became inflamed. Mom asked me to go into the backyard and get some mud to put on her toe. This didn't help at all.

Very quickly Mom's leg started to swell, and then her arm on that same side of her body. She called our neighbor, who was a fireman, to ask him what to do. He said to put straight ammonia on the toe. We tried it, but it didn't stop the swelling. By now Mom was starting to itch horribly, which was the next step of the reaction. I remember my sisters and brother and I just watching our mom and wondering what we could do. We took turns holding our new little baby, and we felt afraid and helpless. Our doctor was unreachable because it was a holiday, but after several telephone calls Mom finally was able to reach another doctor who said to send someone quickly for the medication he would order. Our neighbor turned on his siren and took off for the closest pharmacy. By this time, Mom's throat was feeling tight. I'm not sure if I knew then that this meant she soon wouldn't be able to breathe.

I wanted my dad to be home, and I wanted someone to make everything okay. I went into my parents' room, knelt by the bed, and cried to Heavenly Father. I told him I needed my mom. I told him we had this new baby and that my dad wasn't home, that we were children and didn't know what to do. I also told him that our neighbor had gone for medicine, and I pled with him to bless my mom and to please not let anything happen to her.

I know he heard me. I felt comfort from him. I think I would have felt the same sweet peace no matter how this situation ended. I had said my prayers many times before, but this time I remember so well feeling that he was aware of me and had heard my prayer. I also felt that everything would be okay. And it was. The medicine arrived, the swelling went down, the itching stopped, and my mom was okay. I am grateful that I had been taught that

Heavenly Father hears my prayers. I am so grateful that I knew I could talk with him. And I am grateful that he blessed my mom on that Independence Day when I was nine years old.

So often when we pray, the answer we need most is simply to know that Heavenly Father is close by. Sometimes we need direction or confirmation of decisions we have made. Sometimes we pray for actions to take place, for someone to be healed or something to stop happening. And sometimes we simply need to feel peace. Elder Marvin J. Ashton said, "Who is to say it isn't more important to know he is there than to receive immediate answers." (*New Era*, October 1993, p. 4.) Much of our need can be filled simply by feeling his presence and by being blessed with his peace.

Karen is a young woman who is involved in many extracurricular school activities. Among other things, she is a cheerleader and sings in several elite singing groups. She was feeling overwhelmed and pulled in many directions, and in the midst of this she was feeling criticism from others for not doing things the way they wanted her to do them. Karen knew she couldn't please everyone, and she knew she was really okay, but the emotion of it all caught up with her.

She came home from school one day in tears. She went to her room unable to stop crying. She knelt down and cried to Heavenly Father, asking him to calm her down and help her to know that everything was really okay. As she finished her prayer, she stopped crying and felt calm and peaceful. She reflected on her experience, "Even though there were people that were criticizing me, I knew first of all that Heavenly Father and Jesus loved

me, and that there were people around me—my family
and friends—who loved me and recognized my efforts."
Karen didn't receive any great answer or direction, but
she was blessed with everything she needed, and she felt
peace.

I love this scripture: "Before they call, I will answer;
and while they are yet speaking, I will hear." (Isaiah
65:24.) He is that ready and even eager to hear and
answer us. It is clear that he is aware of each of us and
"knoweth what things [we] have need of, before [we] ask
him." (Matthew 6:8.)

Elder David E. Sorensen clarifies our need to pray
even if Heavenly Father already knows what we would tell
him: "The reason our Heavenly Father asks us to pray
cannot be that we are able to tell him something he does
not already know. Rather, the reason he asks us to pray is
that the process of learning to communicate effectively
with him will shape and change our lives." Elder Sorensen
also stated that "the greatest blessing and benefit is not
the physical or spiritual blessings that may come as
answers to our prayers but in the changes to our soul that
come as we learn to be dependent on our Heavenly
Father for strength. . . . The very act of praying will
improve us." (*Ensign,* May 1993, p. 31.)

It may help to understand that "the object of prayer is
not to change the will of God, but to secure for ourselves
and for others blessings that God is already willing to
grant, but that are made conditional on our asking for
them." (Bible Dictionary, p. 753.) Heavenly Father is willing to grant us many blessings, many of which are dependent upon our asking for them. We need to recognize
that we and Heavenly Father are on the same team. We

can pray sincerely, not to change the will of God but to be more in tune with his will for us and to allow him to be a personal part of our lives.

When my sister Tracy was eleven years old, she fell off the monkey bars on the school playground and broke her back. It was a blessing that it broke in such a way that she had no permanent damage or impairment. She spent several days in the hospital and wore a body cast for six weeks to allow time for healing. The day after her fall, she had to lie still in her hospital bed and wasn't feeling well. She finally said to me, "Can we have a prayer that I can throw up?" I suggested we pray that she feel better, and whatever that took would be fine. I said the prayer, asking Heavenly Father to bless Tracy to feel better and thanking him for watching over her. Within a short time she felt better and was able to rest well. She had the faith to ask, and she knew that Heavenly Father had blessed her to feel better.

We can learn a lot from the Old Testament example of Daniel in the lion's den. The miracle of this story was that the lions did not eat Daniel because he was protected by the Lord. Another important part of the story is the reason Daniel was cast into the den of lions: Daniel refused to stop praying to the Lord when wicked men convinced the king that anyone who "shall ask a petition of any God or man for thirty days" should be cast into a den of lions. When Daniel knew that this decree had been signed, "he kneeled upon his knees three times a day, and prayed, and gave thanks before his God, as he did aforetime." (Daniel 6:10.) Prayer was important to Daniel—important enough that he did not stop praying even though his life was in danger if he did so.

Some years ago I had a choice to make between two

good employment opportunities. Two weeks after I had accepted a job in a new department, I was told that I could return to my former department and take a job I had really wanted for some time. I thanked Heavenly Father for this opportunity to go back and take the job that I really wanted, *and* I asked him to help me do what would be best for me. I was an emotional mess for a week, trying to decide whether to keep my new job or return to my "dream job." I had been told that I could decide which of the opportunities I would take—the choice was mine.

I felt confused, and I kept asking Heavenly Father why he wasn't guiding me. I told him I wanted *my* choice, but I felt torn, and I kept asking him to help me not do the wrong thing. I spent a week of great confusion. I needed to notify others of my decision by 4:30 P.M. on the appointed day. All day long I went between my office, the rest room, and anywhere else I could find solitude, pleading for guidance and saying, "Heavenly Father, why aren't you guiding me? Please help me to make the wisest decision."

At 4:25 P.M. I got off my knees in my office and, not knowing what else to do, called the designated telephone number and said, "I will stay where I am. I cannot feel good about the other option." Immediately I felt peace, and clearly the words came into my mind, "Jamie, do you know what a stupor of thought is?" I had thought Heavenly Father wasn't listening, that he wasn't guiding me. I had kept asking, and my patient Heavenly Father had kept answering me and guiding me the whole time. But I hadn't recognized his answer. He guided me in a way that was best for me and that has been a blessing in my life.

Some would say that this was taking away my agency, but I could have chosen either option. Heavenly Father wasn't making me choose the way he knew would be best for me. I had asked for his guidance, and lovingly and persistently he kept giving it to me.

It is a wonderful process to learn how Heavenly Father communicates with us, and how to recognize answers and direction from him. It may be easier for us to recognize "yes" answers. I learned in my experience that some "no" answers may feel like we are not receiving an answer at all. They can be just as clear and just as real and are given just as lovingly, but we need to learn to recognize them. I think it is good to switch the question around if we think we are not receiving an answer. Then we can have it answered in a positive way: "Your bosom shall burn within you." (D&C 9:8.)

Three-year-old Bradley said to his parents one day, "Heavenly Father doesn't really answer me because he's not really there." He knew that when people talk with each other, they hear each other's voices, so that is how he expected Heavenly Father to answer his prayer. When he didn't hear a voice speaking to him after his prayer, Bradley thought that Heavenly Father wasn't really there. His parents helped him understand that Heavenly Father most often answers our prayers in ways other than speaking to us, but that he is really there. Elder Boyd K. Packer has said, "I have come to know that the voice of inspiration comes more as a feeling than as a sound." (*Ensign*, November 1979, p. 19.)

I was at the home of some friends one evening when it was time for one-year-old Spencer to have a bath and go to bed. Spencer loved to take baths. He was playing intently with a toy in the living room when suddenly he dropped the toy and crawled quickly down the hallway to the other end of the house where his mother was running the bathwater. I hadn't even heard the sound of the running water, but Spencer knew and loved that sound. It was important to him. And he knew what to listen for. Elder Packer explains, "It is difficult to separate from the confusion of life that quiet voice of inspiration. Unless you attune yourself, you will miss it." (*Ensign*, November 1979, p. 19.)

We can learn to listen for and understand the inspiration and guidance Heavenly Father gives to us. He is eager to communicate with us. He does hear and answer our prayers. Our efforts and belief are necessary, but he is there and he is willing. "Ask, and it shall be given unto you; seek, and ye shall find; knock, and it shall be opened unto you. For every one that asketh, receiveth; and he that seeketh, findeth; and to him that knocketh, it shall be opened." (3 Nephi 14:7–8.) We must ask, seek, and knock; when we do, we will receive, find, and it shall be opened.

The promises that come with the command to pray always are great. They include: "Pray always, lest you enter into temptation and lose your reward" (D&C 31:12); "Pray always, that you may come off conqueror; yea, that you may conquer Satan" (D&C 10:5); "Pray always, and I will pour out my Spirit upon you, and great shall be your blessing" (D&C 19:38); and "Pray always, and be believing, and all things shall work together for your good" (D&C 90:24). May we recognize the blessing of prayer in our lives, that these promised blessings may be ours.

CHAPTER SEVEN

"Counsel with the Lord"

I don't remember when I first realized that when we pray, we can tell Heavenly Father how we feel. We don't just need to tell him what we think we are supposed to tell him in a prayer; we can tell him what we are really thinking and feeling. We can tell him the good things and the bad, when it has been a great day and when things are not going so well. We can tell him when we are jealous and angry and when we feel peaceful and happy. He listens, is always there for us, and really understands. He already knows how we feel, but when we tell him, we know that he knows.

"As soon as we learn the true relationship in which we stand toward God (namely, God is our Father, and we are his children), then at once prayer becomes natural and instinctive on our part. . . . Many of the so-called difficulties about prayer arise from forgetting this relationship." (Bible Dictionary, p. 752.) We are blessed to know that he is our Father who loves us unconditionally, who wants the best for us, and who knows what we need and how to bless us. When we really understand this basic truth and recognize the relationship we have with him, we will be ready and anxious to communicate openly with him and gratefully tell him how we feel.

I remember going down to my room to go to bed one night about ten o'clock. My brother Don was out late that evening, and when he came home he had an important message to give to me about something that was happening early the next morning. He couldn't wait until morning to give me the message, so he came into my room to wake me up and give me the information. I had fallen asleep as I was saying my prayers. Don kindly woke me up, and I tried to act as if I was just finishing my prayer. However, it was clear that I had been asleep. My kind brother chuckled and said, "Boy, Jamie. You must really have boring prayers."

Don was right. I probably do have boring prayers sometimes. I have learned since then that we can tell Heavenly Father that we are tired and that we know we will fall asleep soon, so our prayer will be short, but that we love him and recognize him. It is honest and sincere to communicate with him like that, and he knows it is from our hearts. We must remember to be respectful, because we are talking with Heavenly Father. But we can be honest and sincere in a most respectful way as we tell him how we really feel.

Heavenly Father does not think less of us when we tell him less than perfect things or when we tell him of mistakes we have made. He already knows about them. We cannot hide thoughts, feelings, or information from him, even if we don't express them to him, because he knows us so well. That is a little scary until we remember that not only does he know us perfectly, but he also loves us perfectly, and he wants to help and bless us. As we tell him how we feel, even about mistakes we have made, we can be assured that he loves us. That is part of the process of building a meaningful and secure relationship with him.

The way we develop a close relationship with anyone is by sharing our feelings and communicating openly and often. The same is true for our relationship with Heavenly Father.

We probably all have someone we consider to be our best friend. It may be someone in our Young Women group; it may be our mom or our sister; it may even be a boyfriend. What would happen if we talked with our best friend only once a day, just before we went to bed at night. Some nights we may already have crawled into bed and then realize, "Oh, I didn't talk with my best friend today!" We may turn over to go to sleep and say, "I'll talk with her tomorrow," or we may reach over to the telephone on the nightstand or drag ourselves out of bed to the telephone. When our friend answers the telephone, we tell her exactly what we told her the night before, we don't let her react to what we told her, and we don't let her tell us about her day. Then we crawl back into bed and don't even think about our best friend until the next night just as we are going to bed. I wonder how long we would be best friends?

Does this sound at all like the way we communicate with Heavenly Father? We sometimes remember to say our prayers just before going to bed, and then we don't think about him until the next night when we tell him exactly what we told him the night before. If he is really our Heavenly Father who knows us so well and loves us so much, then he is eager to bless our lives—but we need to do our part. We can cast "all [our] care upon him; for he careth for [us]." (1 Peter 5:7.) We can "cry unto the Lord" (Alma 34:27) and "pour out [our] souls" unto him (Alma 34:26). We can "cry unto God for all [our] support" (Alma 37:36) and "counsel with the Lord in all [our] doings, and he will direct [us] for good" (Alma 37:37).

Let's think about how we would answer this question asked by President Ezra Taft Benson: "When you pray—when you talk to your Heavenly Father—do you really talk out your problems with him? Do you let him know your feelings, your doubts, your insecurities, your joys, your deepest desires—or is prayer merely an habitual expression with the same words and phrases?" (*Ensign*, November 1977, p. 32.)

Here is another question posed by Elder William R. Bradford: "Do I have time for prayer? I don't mean just an occasional, quick, repetitious prayer that is like giving a wave of the hand to your Father in Heaven as you pass him on your way to something important. I mean sincere, honest, 'from the depths of a contrite spirit and a broken heart' prayer; kneeling in humility, demonstrating to the Holy Father that you really love him; private prayer which involves you in the process of repentance and pleading for forgiveness and allows time for pondering and waiting for the answers to come." (*Ensign*, May 1992, p. 28.) We have the opportunity of literally communicating with our Heavenly Father. Certainly nothing else is so important that it should keep us from doing so.

Six-and-a-half-year-old Elizabeth came downstairs at eight o'clock on Thanksgiving morning. Most of the others in the family were taking advantage of the chance to sleep in on a cold autumn holiday. Elizabeth's mother mentioned to Elizabeth that she was the first child in the family to wake up and noted that she was up early for a holiday. Elizabeth replied, "I have really been up since seven-thirty. But first I made my bed and then I said my morning prayers. And that took quite a while today." Her mother asked Elizabeth what she had talked about in her prayer. She humbly and shyly responded, "Lots of the same things I talked about in family prayer last night. And I asked Heavenly Father to bless the homeless."

Surely Heavenly Father heard that sincere prayer of a six-year-old. Does it take us "quite a while" to talk with him about the things we are grateful for, how we are feeling, what we desire, and to ask him to bless others who are in need? I hope we begin our day the way Elizabeth begins hers.

I love the words Enos used to describe his experience of "mighty prayer." The words include "wrestle" (Enos 1:2), "my soul hungered," "I cried unto him in mighty prayer and supplication," "all the day long did I cry unto him," "when the night came I did still raise my voice high that it reached the heavens" (v. 4), "struggling in the spirit," and "prayed and labored with all diligence" (v. 10). These are strong words. Are they different from the words we would use to describe our prayers? This kind of faith and communication resulted in a powerful experience for Enos: "There came a voice unto me, saying: Enos, thy sins are forgiven thee, and thou shalt be blessed" (Enos 1:5), and "Behold, the voice of the Lord came into my mind again" (v. 10), and "the Lord said unto me . . . " (v. 12). These same results could be ours if we put forth the same kind of effort that Enos did and follow his example of sincere communication with Heavenly Father.

Elder Loren C. Dunn observed: "Sometimes we compartmentalize. We pray about one thing and worry about something else. We seem to limit the ability of the Lord to help us in every aspect of our lives." (*Ensign,* May 1981, p. 25.) There is nothing he is unaware of in our lives and nothing that he is unable to help us with.

One day in February, four-year-old Alex had to take two very important things with him to preschool. One was a paper signed by his mother; the other was a pile of valentines for his friends. He had spent hours carefully signing his own name to each of the valentines. Alex and his mom were rushing to get to preschool on time. As they were going out the door, Alex remembered the paper and valentines. His mother quickly searched the house, looking for both but finding neither. Alex said, "Mom, maybe we should pray." His mother kept searching; then she thought of a new place to look and found the paper. Alex exclaimed, "It worked! It worked! I didn't think it would work, but it did. I prayed and we found it!"

Time was short, and the valentines were still not to be found. Alex suggested that they try praying again. His mother had decided they should just leave the valentines home because they were running so late, and she was afraid for Alex's faith if he prayed again and the valentines were not found. On her way out the door she thought of one more cupboard she had not looked in. She went to it—and there were the valentines. "It worked again! I didn't think it would, but it did! I prayed again, and it worked!" Alex exclaimed. Nothing is too insignificant for Heavenly Father. If it is important to us, it is important to him.

We can pray about whatever is happening in our lives and whatever is important to us right now. There are some things that we probably always pray for. Elder Vaughn J. Featherstone has said, "Of the last thousand prayers that I have offered, the above items [family, Church leaders, missionaries, the leaders of our country] would have been prayed for a thousand times." (*Charity Never Faileth* [Salt Lake City: Deseret Book Co., 1980], p. 70.) He calls this "sincere repetition," and it is most appropriate when we pray. But we can also tell Heavenly Father what is happening in our lives at this very moment. There are no limits to his ability to bless our lives—except the limitations we create by not recognizing his ability to bless our lives.

Let's go back to the scripture "Counsel with the Lord in all thy doings, and he will direct thee for good." (Alma 37:37.) *Counsel* means more than to talk or tell. I like the definition that reads, "Discussion, deliberation, consultation." (*Webster's Third New International Dictionary*, s.v. "counsel.") If we truly counsel with Heavenly Father, we will discuss, deliberate, and consult with him. We will tell him how we feel, then pause and think about it while we are still on our knees. We will pay attention to thoughts and feelings that will come. We will tell him why we think we feel the way we feel and talk about the new thoughts and feelings, then pause, again paying attention to new ideas, thoughts, and feelings that will come. He will speak to us through our thoughts and feelings, for he has told us, "I will tell you in your mind and in your heart." (D&C 8:2.) When we pray in this way, we are doing more than saying our prayers—we are communicating with Heavenly Father.

We can follow this process no matter what we are praying about: when we are lonely, when we are having a hard time in school, when there is contention in our home, when we are concerned about the pressures of the world and the temptations are strong, when we feel we shouldn't date the same boy quite so often, when we want to really study the Book of Mormon and know if it is true, when we don't like ourselves very well, when we need to feel peace, and when we desire to know if Heavenly Father really loves us and if there really is a Plan. This deeper-than-surface communication will give us a greater feeling of closeness to Heavenly Father. It will bring nearer to our minds and memories the premortal, loving relationship we had with him.

Not all of our prayers will be "counseling" prayers. We are still communicating with him whenever we pray—when our prayers are short, when we thank him for blessings, and when we ask him for things we need. He hears and answers those prayers too. However, there will be times in each of our lives when the only way to receive what we need to receive and feel what we need to feel is by counseling with the Lord and communicating as Enos did when he "prayed and labored with all diligence." (Enos 1:12.)

I feel such love for Heavenly Father as I think of these things and recognize how blessed we are to know that he lives, that he is close to us, and that we can communicate with him. He knows us well and loves us unconditionally even when we don't communicate with him. But unless we make the effort and seek him sincerely, we may not feel that love regularly or know that often he is close to us.

I know a three-year-old who says in every prayer she offers, "Heavenly Father, please bless Heavenly Father." It warms my heart when I hear her ask for such a blessing. I think what she means is, "Heavenly Father, you are real to me. I love you, and you are one I think about often." She prays for her family and for others she loves, and Heavenly Father is among those she loves the most. May our relationship with him be a personal relationship of complete trust, in which we sincerely tell him how we feel and counsel with him. As we do this, he will counsel with us, and we will know that he understands how we feel.

CHAPTER EIGHT

Find Yourself—Be Yourself

On a trip to southern California, my sisters, a friend, and I had only half a day of vacation left before we would fly home to Utah late in the afternoon. We had rented a car and were planning on spending the afternoon with an uncle in Los Angeles, then arriving at the airport in time to return the rental car and catch our flight home. It didn't work out quite the way we thought it would. To put it simply, we got lost.

It was like one of those dreams in which you try and try but cannot get where you want to go. We didn't expect to have any trouble finding Uncle Don's house. We had been there before. We kept calling him from pay telephones, telling him where we were, and he would give us more directions to find his home. We went in circles, we went in the wrong direction, and several times we went right past where we wanted to be. His directions seemed clear, and each time we would call him he was surprised at where we were calling from. We were losing time and soon became less concerned about missing the wonderful meal Uncle Don had prepared and more concerned about finding the airport in time to catch our plane.

Finally, we found Uncle Don's house with only enough time to run up his front steps and receive his kindly handwritten instructions leading us a step at a time to the airport. We barely (I mean barely) arrived in time to check our luggage and board the plane. Being that lost was frustrating and frightening. We had good instructions, and we were trying hard, but we just couldn't find our way.

We probably all have times when we feel that we are lost—we may wonder *where* we are and *who* we are. That can be a scary and lonely feeling, yet it can be a wonderful opportunity for self-discovery. It is one of the greatest adventures of life to find ourselves and one of the greatest challenges to be ourselves. It may take some driving in circles and even going in the wrong direction for a time. There will probably be times when we will feel lost. But it can be a great journey, and the destination will be worth it.

We can't talk about finding ourselves and being ourselves without first recognizing that we are worth finding and being, simply because we are daughters of God. There is purpose in our lives and things Heavenly Father needs us each to do. If we don't find ourselves and be ourselves, who will do those things we could have done? Who will contribute those things we could have contributed? Finding ourselves may involve quite a search, or we may need only to be pointed in the right direction. Either way, our Heavenly Father is there to bless us, help us find ourselves, and help us feel good about who we find.

The word *find* may sound almost accidental, but there is really nothing accidental about our lives and who we will be. Finding, in this sense, involves a wonderful process of discovering and creating. It includes discovering talents, abilities, interests, hopes, and desires and creating from among them the person we will be.

We need to remember something obvious but important in this process of finding, creating, and being ourselves. Leo Buscaglia said it so well: "If you try to be like anyone else, you may come very close, but you will always be second best. But, you are the best you. It is the easiest, most practical, most rewarding thing to be." (*Love* [New York: Fawcett Crest, 1972], p. 143.) We will never be anyone else, no matter how hard we try. We will never live anyone's life but our own, no matter how hard we wish to. When we realize that we are who we will always be, we can focus our energies on finding, discovering, and creating, and it will be a most rewarding adventure.

Part of creating is to look at the good qualities we see in others and to learn from them and develop similar qualities in our own lives. When we see wonderful things in others' lives that we wish we had or that we wish we were, we need not become discouraged. We can be happy for those people and glad for their example, then apply the good things we learn from them into our own lives as those things apply to being us. We can add to who we are to become better, but we need to be ourselves.

I have a friend who is five feet four inches tall. I think that would be a great height to be, but she has always dreamed of being taller and very slender. She is energetic and takes good care of her body but somehow hasn't been satisfied with what she has had to work with. One day after she had energetically jogged her usual five to six miles, she made a marvelous discovery and exclaimed, "Guess what! I will never have long skinny legs!" That seemed clear to me already, but for her it was a great awakening to the fact that she was who she was. With this awareness, she accepted who she was and hasn't worried about not having long skinny legs since.

That reminds me of the scripture that points out that there are some things we cannot change just by wishing: "Which of you by taking thought can add one cubit unto his stature?" (Matthew 6:27.) There may be some things we can't change about ourselves (like the length of our legs), but we can accept those things, be happy, and work with them to our best advantage.

A sure way to not accept ourselves is to compare ourselves with others. That can be especially discouraging when we compare what we don't have with the good things that someone else does have. Remember, Heavenly Father does not compare us with anyone else. He doesn't grade on a curve, and he doesn't expect or even want us to be everything—he wants us to be our best selves. He has said, "All have not every gift given unto them; for there are many gifts, and to every man is given a gift by the Spirit of God." (D&C 46:11.) He expects us to and will help us to develop our individual gifts.

At times we may try to feel better about who we are by criticizing others we see as being better or "higher" than we are. We "lower" others in our minds or try to make them feel lower about themselves because we think that will make us feel "higher" and better about ourselves. When we do this, we will never get the results we are seeking. We cannot think negatively or say unkind things about someone and still feel peaceful and good about ourselves. "Let us therefore follow after the things which make for peace, and things wherewith one may edify another." (Romans 14:19.) Edifying others is one of the most satisfying qualities to find and develop in ourselves. When we do, we will feel good about ourselves and others as well.

We will undoubtedly find in our lives that there is more to us than we know about right now. Finding those undiscovered parts will be exciting, broadening, and eye-opening.

When I was in high school, I enjoyed participating in athletics more than I enjoyed studying, sleeping, dating, or doing the more domestic things that some girls did. I thought the athletic part of my life was me, but I discovered that it was only part of me. During my senior year, I was surprised with an award for being the top student from my school in home economics. It was a great shock because home economics was a lot of things that I wasn't. My biggest concern was that I might have to miss a basketball practice in order to attend the state home economics competition. In spite of my doubts, I learned some new skills, found some abilities I had had all along, and developed others I had known a little about.

Being named a finalist in the state competition was less of a shock than receiving my first award, because by the time of the state competition I had found that home economics could be a part of my life and was part of being me. I decided I could play basketball, then sew a dress, make a pastry, and shoot more free throws. It is a wonderful discovery to find and create new parts to our lives.

Part of finding ourselves and being ourselves is believing in ourselves and dreaming a little bit. How many times do we hear people say, "Oh, I could never do that," or "I wish I could do that." We need to believe that we can do new things, things we have never done before. We need to make efforts to learn, to practice, and to get good at something we want to be good at. My friend Kathy had a dream to oil paint, but she doubted that she would be very good. It was only a dream until our artist friend Dot said, "Then do it! Why don't you do it if you really want to?" Dot showed her some basics, and Kathy committed to take lessons. Her home and many others are now beautifully decorated with Kathy's paintings.

Not everyone who dreams of being an Olympic champion will win a gold medal, but many people can fill their lives with growth, accomplishments, and personal triumphs because they reach for that dream anyway. When four-year-old Melissa gracefully dances around the family room copying every move of the world-champion ice dancers, she is dreaming of being the best. She will start a dance class soon, and that is the beginning of her dream, even if she never performs outside of her family room.

Another part of finding and being ourselves is to do things *we* enjoy doing, even if everyone else is doing other things. I attended a Young Women Evening of Excellence and was impressed when one of the participants demonstrated her karate skills. She had received numerous awards and was very good. She had obviously committed herself to many hours of practice. This young woman was the only one out of a large group who had this interest and who had worked hard to be good at it. I had never even thought of learning karate, but I respected her skills greatly and her desire to do something she wanted to do even if everyone else was doing other things.

I know a twelve-year-old named Anne who loves Shakespeare. She has read more of Shakespeare's works in her young life than I have even heard of. She has memorized favorite speeches and even dressed like Henry V for Halloween. I admire her for doing what she loves even if few other twelve-year-olds like to do the same thing.

We know that our worth is already within us because we are daughters of God. Skills and interests don't add to our worth, but they help us be all we can be and reach the potential that is within us. I believe that many people are given gifts that they need to recognize and develop. Finding those gifts and developing them is part of the plan Heavenly Father has for us. I have a friend who plays the piano beautifully. She has practiced hard for many years to develop this talent. When she is complimented on her ability, she responds, "It is a gift." Her effort has been great, but she recognizes the gift of talent given to her by her Heavenly Father.

I love the challenge I hear and the wise counsel we receive in this statement by Elder Robert L. Backman: "Life sometimes has a way of beating us down until we want to be comfortable instead of excellent, until we'd like to rest instead of run the rapids. You know how it goes. You start as a young person thinking you'd like to be brilliant at something, and then you find out how much work it would be. You discover that excellence is painful, that high standards mean hard labor. So you rethink your standards and give yourself grand excuses. 'I guess I'm just an average kind of guy,' you say to yourself. That sounds all right until you remember that average is

66

as close to the bottom as it is to the top. . . . With every choice in life, we are not merely choosing things or events. We are choosing ourselves, for just as surely as we shape life, it shapes us." (*Be Master of Yourself* [Salt Lake City: Deseret Book Co., 1986], p. 7.)

We do choose ourselves, and we do shape our lives. We don't need to limit ourselves. We can try new things, expand our interests, develop new skills, and enlarge our positive qualities. Someone has said, "The best in you is better than you think!" We can find the best in ourselves and develop it and enjoy being who we are. As we find ourselves, we become unique. I think that is exciting! That makes us each one of a kind, and "one-of-a-kinds" are very valuable.

May we recognize, with Heavenly Father's help and direction, that our lives are worth finding and developing and worth living fully. He knows who we are and who we can become, and with his help we will discover this too.

CHAPTER NINE

Think the Right Thoughts

*O*ne hot summer Sunday I was having one of those days when I did not feel good about myself and when I did not feel that Heavenly Father loved me either. Those two things often go together, because when we don't feel lovable we cannot imagine even Heavenly Father loving us. I had been to my church meetings that morning and noticed how nice everyone else looked. My hair had curled funny, and I was sure everyone had noticed. So-and-so played the piano well—she is much more talented than I am. And another so-and-so sure had a cute guy with her today, and hey, it's not fair that I didn't have a cute guy to sit by in church. After my meetings, I finished the things I needed to do for my calling, then drove home and went for a walk.

I was walking down a street in my neighborhood with my hands in my pockets, probably looking very solemn and unhappy. I was feeling bad, but at the same time I had a prayer in my heart: "Heavenly Father, please help me to feel better about myself, to know that I am better than I feel right now, and to know that I am loved by thee." As I approached a corner near a busy street, something surprising happened. Driving on the busy street was a beat-up red pickup truck. The driver of the truck made a U-turn, pulled onto the street on which I was walking, made another U-turn, and pulled up right beside me.

I kept walking because I was deep in my own thoughts, and when I realized what was happening I felt nervous. The truck kept moving right along beside me. With one hand on the steering wheel, the driver leaned over to the passenger side of the truck and unrolled the window. Then he yelled something to me. I glanced over to see an elderly man whom I had never seen before. I kept walking and tried to ignore the man and the truck still moving along beside me as I walked. The man again yelled something to me. This time I turned to him in a you-are-bothering-me tone of voice and said, "What?"

He cheerily asked, "Why don't you smile?"

I emphatically responded, "I'm thinking!"

His quick response was, "If you'd think the right thoughts you could smile! Love ya!" The man rolled up the window and drove back out onto the busy street.

My first thought was, "Who in the world does that old man think he is to tell me to smile!" I felt feisty and offended that someone would intrude upon my thoughts like that. Then I realized what I had been thinking. I was comparing myself to others. I was thinking about little negative things that no one else had noticed anyway, and even if they had it wouldn't really matter. And I was far away from thinking (and feeling) that Heavenly Father loved me. I had been praying in my heart that I would feel better, and my "guardian angel" came driving up in a beat-up red pickup truck reminding me that Heavenly

Father is aware of me, that he does answer my prayers, and that if I do think the right thoughts I can smile and be happy!

To a great degree the thoughts we think will determine how we feel and whether we will be happy or not. By changing our thoughts we can often be happy when we thought we were unhappy. We have the power to choose what we think. By having this power, we not only choose our thoughts and our feelings, but ultimately we choose our lives. President Spencer W. Kimball once said, "A man is literally what he thinks, his character being the complete sum of all his thoughts." (*The Miracle of Forgiveness* [Salt Lake City: Bookcraft, 1969], p. 103.) W. H. Davies, a British poet, also spoke wisely: "No matter where [the] body is, the mind is free to go elsewhere." ("The Mind's Liberty," in *Modern British Poetry*, edited by Louis Untermeyer [New York: Harcourt, Brace & World, 1962], p. 178.) That can be good or bad, but the point is, we decide.

We must remember that Heavenly Father "knows all the thoughts and intents of the heart." (Alma 18:32.) He also has the power and desire to guide, bless, and strengthen us as we try to control our thoughts. He will give us great blessings as our minds are focused on those things that would allow us to receive those blessings. We will even be blessed to "feast upon his love; for [we] may, if [our] minds are firm, forever." (Jacob 3:2.)

Satan wants us to think negative thoughts and to let our minds go wherever they happen to wander. He is the one who rules in those places where there is no self-control. He knows that if he can get us to think negative thoughts, we will feel negative, and he likes that. He has then increased the odds that we will do negative things, and he likes that too.

As a youth I heard Elder Boyd K. Packer talk about our minds being like a stage. There is always something on that stage, and it is up to each of us to be in control of what scenes we will allow. If something negative or unworthy comes on the stage, we can replace it. We *must* replace it. There will always be something there, but we must make a conscious effort to decide what it will be. (See *Ensign,* January 1974, p. 28.) We want to be in control of our lives. If we do not decide what we will think, then the influences of the world and the subtleties of Satan will decide for us. It takes more than just not allowing negative or obscene thoughts. We must also consciously direct and control our thoughts in uplifting and positive ways.

President David O. McKay spoke a profound truth when he said, "I will know what you are if you will tell me what you think about when you don't have to think." (*True to the Faith: Sermons and Writings of David O. McKay,* compiled by Llewelyn R. McKay [Salt Lake City: Bookcraft, 1966], p. 270.) That scares me just a bit. What *do* we think about when we don't have to think?

I was baby-sitting my nephews Jeff and Jared and their baby sister Michelle. We had enjoyed a fun evening together. The boys had brushed their teeth and said their prayers. I had tucked them into bed and was in the next room rocking Michelle. I thought the boys were asleep when I heard four-year-old Jeff say to two-year-old Jared, "Hey, Jared, do you know who the first man on earth was?"

Silence . . . "Uh-uh."

Then Jeff said, "It was Adam."

"Oh, yeah," was Jared's reply.

The discussion continued as Jeff said, "Jared, do you know who the first woman was?"

Silence . . . "Uh-uh."

The big brother said, "It was Eve."

"Oh, yeah," said Jared. I thought the conversation was over; then I realized they were just thinking.

Jared asked the next question: "Hey, Jeff, who were the first kids?"

Jeff seemed surprised by the question. "I don't know," he said.

Silence. Then Jeff had the answer: "Jared, I know. They were Adam and Eve's kids!"

Now, there is really nothing profound about that story. We probably knew the story of Adam and Eve when we were two- and four-year-olds too. The thing that impressed me was what these little boys were thinking about as they lay in bed that night. I am sure there were many happenings of the day and excitements about tomorrow upon which their minds could have rested. Instead they were thinking about spiritual things, even letting "the solemnities of eternity rest upon [their] minds." (D&C 43:34.)

We probably all know people who sing their favorite hymn or repeat a memorized scripture when they need to change their negative thoughts to something positive. Whenever I hear a certain friend of mine humming the tune to the Primary song "My Heavenly Father Loves Me," I know she is wanting to change her thoughts to something positive. We need to do whatever works for each of us so we can be in control of what we let into our minds.

We mess up a lot of todays by regretting our yesterdays and worrying about our tomorrows. We need to learn from our yesterdays and plan our tomorrows, but we need to focus our energies and our thoughts on living well today. I think we also carry around some unnecessary burdens, many of which could be lifted simply by changing our thoughts. These burdens include self-doubts, insecurities, and fears that weigh us down and cloud the clear vision of who we really are. We wouldn't have those doubts and fears unless we were thinking things that allow those feelings to enter and fester. We can replace those thoughts with positive thoughts and replace the negative feelings with peace. That is not brainwashing ourselves or being unrealistic; it is helping us gain control of our lives.

I have a friend named Laura who told me of a time when she was feeling down on herself. A friend suggested that she write down all of the negative things she was thinking about herself and then tear up the list and throw it away. Laura made her list of negatives; then she decided she would make a list of positive things she could find about herself. The positive list was not nearly as long as the negative list. She didn't throw the negative list away but folded it up and put it away, deciding that she wanted to concentrate on her positive list.

Laura said that within a couple of weeks she made a complete turnaround about how she felt. She had made a conscious effort to think good things, and amazingly enough she began to believe them and to feel good about who she was. Sometime later she pulled out the negative list. By then she was feeling good about herself, and she was surprised that she had really thought those negative things. She commented, "No one is really as bad as those things I was thinking about myself." It does take effort, but if the choice is between feeling good or bad, which do we choose?

Sometimes negative thoughts come because we are worried or concerned about things in our lives. Some of those things are concerns over which we have no control, but we can still get through times of worry and concern if our thoughts are controlled and focused on being positively at peace instead of dropping deeper into despair. I love this counsel from Philippians: "Don't be unduly concerned about anything," reads the footnote definition, "but in every thing by prayer and supplication with thanksgiving let your requests be made known unto God. And the peace of God, which passeth all understanding, shall keep your hearts and minds through Christ Jesus." (4:6–7.) "Don't be unduly concerned" means to not be excessively concerned. When things are out of our control, we can seek Heavenly Father through prayer with thanksgiving, and the promise of his peace is ours.

What do we think about Heavenly Father? *Do* we think about Heavenly Father? "For how knoweth a man the master whom he has not served, and who is a stranger unto him, and is far from the thoughts and intents of his heart?" (Mosiah 5:13.) I hope he is not far from the thoughts of our hearts. We are very much a part of the thoughts of his heart. Thinking about him, his blessings to us, and his teachings are certainly peaceful places on which to rest our minds.

I have found that if I go to bed at night with positive, peaceful things on my mind, then I wake up feeling that same way. Why not let our last thoughts of the night be turned to Heavenly Father in prayer. In fact, we are told in scripture, "Let all thy thoughts be directed unto the Lord; yea, let the affections of thy heart be placed upon the Lord forever. . . . Yea, when thou liest down at night lie down unto the Lord, that he may watch over you in your sleep; and when thou risest in the morning let thy heart be full of thanks unto God." (Alma 37:36–37.) The promise given with these verses is, "If ye do these things, ye shall be lifted up at the last day." (Alma 37:37.) I love the focus these verses give of being fully directed in our minds and our hearts to Heavenly Father.

The scriptures leave no doubt as to where our minds should be. "Look unto me in every thought; doubt not, fear not." (D&C 6:36.) The promised blessings of this kind of focus are great. They include: "Thou wilt keep him in perfect peace, whose mind is stayed on thee: because he trusteth in thee" (Isaiah 26:3) and "Let virtue garnish thy thoughts unceasingly; then shall thy confidence wax strong in the presence of God" (D&C 121:45). Imagine having "perfect peace" and "confidence in the presence of God." These great blessings are ours as we do those things required to receive them.

A very basic way Heavenly Father communicates with us is through our thoughts. He literally speaks to us through our own minds: "Behold, I will tell you in your mind and in your heart." (D&C 8:2.) Thoughts can come clearly to us that we know are from him if the everyday thoughts we allow into our minds are such that his voice would be comfortable with them. Our minds need to be on the right wavelength to receive his voice. We need to learn to recognize his voice above our own thoughts and other voices that speak to us. The thoughts that come from his voice are most often coupled with feelings of peace and sure knowledge.

It would be a wonderful scripture study to search for verses about our minds, our thoughts, and our hearts. So many verses speak of our minds (or thoughts) and our hearts together. That is because the things we think about (our minds) are directly related to the things that are important to us (our hearts). As we think about changing and controlling our thoughts, we need to consider our hearts—what is important to us in our lives—and perhaps reconsider what we really want to be most important to us.

Elder Gene R. Cook has said, "You cannot rise higher than your own beliefs and thoughts about yourself." ("Trust in The Lord", *Brigham Young University 1983–84 Fireside and Devotional Speeches* [Provo, Utah: BYU Press, 1984], p. 128.) If we think we can move forward in life with confidence, then we can. If we are thinking we can't go forward with confidence, then we won't—not because we can't but because we won't. We can if we think we can.

Let our positive thoughts and faith carry us forward to be who our Heavenly Father knows we really are. We can be among those who think they can. We will then be among those who do. "Behold, the Lord requireth the heart and a *willing* mind." (D&C 64:34; emphasis added.) May our minds be willing, and may we be *willing* to change our minds when we need to.

The greatest of all blessings will be ours as we bring our minds closer to the mind of God. "Sanctify yourselves that your minds become single to God, and the days will come that you shall see him." (D&C 88:68.) What greater blessing can there be? It is available and promised to each of us.

CHAPTER TEN

Don't Follow the World

*O*ne summer, my friends Connie and Peggy and I took a trip to California. We did the usual touristy things, including spending several days at the beach. It was at the beach that people could really tell that we were tourists. Our white legs and fluorescent orange air mattresses (instead of surfboards) were the best clues.

One of the beautiful clear days at the beach found Connie and me daring each other to "ride the waves." So we blew up the air mattresses and bravely headed to the water. We started out cautiously, making sure we could touch our feet to the sandy floor beneath the water. Just as a wave was about to crest, we would jump stomach-down onto the air mattresses and let the wave carry us back to shore. We got pretty daring and ventured out a bit farther where the waves crested higher and the ride was longer. We felt very adventurous, even on fluorescent air mattresses. After a little while and several lungfuls of ocean water, we decided to take a break and go back to where we had left Peggy sitting on the beach.

We walked out of the water and directly up to the

shore to where we thought we had left Peggy. But she wasn't there. The beach was crowded, but we knew about how far from the water we had been when we had sat on our towels before the "catch a wave" scene. We were puzzled not to find Peggy right there. We looked around the area, then up and down the sandy beach, but we still couldn't see her. Finally, a little way down the beach, we saw Lifeguard Station #9. We had remembered sitting right by Lifeguard Station #9 because we had remembered the cute, suntanned lifeguard sitting there. But why were we so far away from it now?

We tucked our air mattresses under our arms and walked up the shore past Lifeguard Station #9 to where Peggy was sitting with our towels, right where we had left her. I wondered how we had moved that far away from where we had begun and from where we wanted to end up. I vaguely remember now having learned in my eighth-grade science class that often the waves of the sea do not come in straight, but they may come into the shore at an angle. It has to do with gravity, winds, and even storms far out at sea. We had been carried down the shore without even realizing it. The next time we "rode the waves," we walked a few feet up the shore each time we were brought by the waves onto the sandy beach. We kept focused on Lifeguard Station #9 (and that cute, suntanned lifeguard) so we would be where we wanted to be and not where the waves of the sea would take us.

The world is much like the waves of the sea. Without knowing it, we can easily be moved far away from where we began and from where we want to end up. We can be carried so subtly that we may move quite a distance before we are frightened by the fact that we are not where we intended to be. Unless we consciously decide for ourselves where we are going, the world will decide for us, because the waves of the world are so strong and convincing. A lack of firm decision may mean that we will be "tossed to and fro, and carried about with every wind of doctrine" (Ephesians 4:14), going wherever the world chooses to take us. Our lives have more meaning than that. We have more power to choose than that, "for the power is in [us], wherein [we] are agents unto [our]selves." (D&C 58:28.)

We must keep focused on the "lifeguard," who is, of course, our Heavenly Father. He is there for each of us, and his love for us is sure. He watches us as we fight against the waves of the world. He is there to save us as we reach out to him against the force of the tides and as we call to him above the roar of the waves. He will bless each of us with strength and perspective to enjoy the ride now and to keep focused on where we want to be when the ride is over.

Power and strength will come to us as we remember we are Heavenly Father's daughters and as we ask him for strength to stand firmly. I love the scripture that talks about building our house upon a rock or upon the sand. The winds and the rains come to all, just as temptations in this life come to all, but if our foundation is firmly built upon a rock we will stand firm when those floods and winds and rains come. (3 Nephi 14:24–27.)

An important part of the foundation on which we must build is our knowledge that "we are daughters of our Heavenly Father who loves us, and we love him" (Young Women Theme.) When we believe that this is true, we better understand that there is great value and purpose to our lives. We also know that there is strength available to us to stand apart from the world and to be who we choose to be, not who the world or people in the world would convince us to be.

Our friends, who may try to convince us to do things that the world is doing, are Heavenly Father's sons and daughters too. They have lived with him, they are "part of his great plan" ("Walk Tall, You're a Daughter of God"), and they will return to him too. He knows each of them, he loves each of them, and he knows their hearts just as he knows ours. It is worth it for us to stand up and let them know what we stand for, to remind them that their lives have great worth too. They have lived with Heavenly Father, and they also chose his plan. If those "friends" reject us for standing firm, we can be comforted knowing that it is better to be acceptable to the Lord than to be accepted by our peers. Sister Michaelene P. Grassli has stated this so well: "It is comforting to me to know that I need only be concerned that what I do and say is acceptable and pleasing to the Lord." (As quoted by Virginia H. Pearce, *Ensign,* November 1992, p. 91.)

President Spencer W. Kimball gave powerful encouragement to the youth of the Church: "In these days directly ahead of you is the decisive decision. Are you going to yield to the easy urge to follow the crowd, or are you going to raise your head above the crowd and let them follow you? Are you going to slip off into mediocrity, or are you going to rise to the heights which your Heavenly Father set for you? You could stand above the crowd and become a leader among your people so that some day they would call your name blessed, or you can follow the usual demands and urges and desires and lose yourself in the herd of millions of folks who do not rise to their potential. The decision is yours and yours only. No one else can fashion and order your life." (*Teachings of Spencer W. Kimball* [Salt Lake City: Bookcraft, 1982], p. 147.)

Sometimes we think that in order to be among the strong and the tough we need to follow the world. Some think that it is weak to have standards and to set limits, and that being good means we have no strength to be ourselves. The truth is that it is the weak, easy, and wishy-washy way to follow the world. It doesn't take any strength or backbone to bend to the pressures and ways of the world.

President Gordon B. Hinckley has said, "Prove your strength, show your independence, by saying no when enticement from peers comes your way." (*Ensign*, May 1987, p. 48.) Real strength comes by standing firm and being who we really are, even if it means standing alone. Real independence means using our agency to think clearly and make wise decisions, not rebelling against the counsel of our parents and others who love us. It means using our agency to do the things that are really best for us, not the things that are most popular.

One Sunday, a Young Women president was teaching a lesson on standing for truth and righteousness to the young women in her ward. Elizabeth was a new Beehive. The president asked Elizabeth to help her for a moment and come to the front of the room. She walked to the front and stood beside the president. They stood side by side. With her hand on Elizabeth's shoulder, the president turned to Elizabeth and asked, "Elizabeth, what are you standing for?"

Elizabeth was puzzled but said, "Because you told me to come up and stand here."

The president countered, "I know, but what are you standing for?"

Elizabeth answered again, "I don't know why you asked me to stand here."

The president may have appeared unsympathetic, and some probably felt like she was putting Elizabeth on the spot. The president asked again, "But Elizabeth, what are you standing for?"

Elizabeth hesitated this time, obviously not sure what answer was expected. Then a sure look came into her eyes, her shoulders straightened, and she seemed to become taller as she responded firmly, "I am standing for truth and righteousness!"

What a marvelous motto for young women: "Stand for truth and righteousness." Let that be our motto. Let there be no doubt as to where and for what we stand. I have heard Sister Ardeth Kapp say on more than one occasion, "If you don't know what you stand for, you will fall for anything."

Part of the Plan was for us to come to this earth and live in the world. We know the answer to the question, "Know ye not that the friendship of the world is enmity with God?" (James 4:4.) The more closely we follow the world, the farther away we are from Heavenly Father. The opposite is also clear: If we are seeking and following Heavenly Father, we will not be living the ways of the world.

The scriptures teach that we are not to follow the world but to "overcome the world" (D&C 63:47), "be not conformed to this world" (Romans 12:2), "keep [ourselves] unspotted from the world" (D&C 59:9), "love not the world, neither the things that are in the world" (1 John 2:15), not "live after the manner of the world" (D&C 95:13), and "lay aside the things of this world, and seek for the things of a better" (D&C 25:10). The *better* world offers the meaningful and eternal things of Heavenly Father. Those things are infinitely *better* than the temporary things that the world can offer.

Katharine, a Laurel, asked one Sunday if she could give the thought in Young Women. She stood in front of this group of her peers and told them that she wanted to share with them something she had learned. She said that she used to think watching R-rated movies was no big deal, that everyone did it, and that the movies would have no negative effect on her. She had been watching such movies as a regular part of her life. She then bore testimony that we have been counseled correctly by our parents and Church leaders not to watch movies that are not in keeping with the standards of the Church and the teachings of Heavenly Father. She told the girls she had realized that watching R-rated movies was affecting her negatively, that she was thinking about things that were not wholesome, and that they were taking her away from feeling good about herself and being close to Heavenly Father. She committed herself to eliminate such movies from her life and admonished the others to do the same. Katharine recognized that the world's ways were not her ways and was willing to help others learn from her experience.

There are many examples in the scriptures of those who chose to seek and follow Heavenly Father instead of following the world. The story of Shadrach, Meshach, and Abed-nego can teach us important things we need today. These three young men refused to worship a golden image (the world), so they were cast into a fiery furnace. But Heavenly Father "delivered his servants that trusted in him" (Daniel 3:28), and he will do the same for us today.

I love the way Peter and the other apostles stood firm in doing what they knew to be right. They were arrested and cast into prison because they had been teaching about Jesus Christ. After they were delivered from prison by an angel, they continued to testify of Jesus. They were again called before the council of chief priests and chastised for their teachings. Their response was, "We ought to obey God rather than men." (Acts 5:29.) After being beaten, they were set free with the command "that they should not speak in the name of Jesus." (Acts 5:40.) Their reaction was to depart "rejoicing that they were counted worthy to suffer shame for his name. And daily in the temple, and in every house, they ceased not to teach and preach Jesus Christ." (Acts 5:41–42.) Their commitment to the things they knew to be right and true was stronger than any pressure from the world. Our commitment to the things we know to be right and true needs to be stronger than any pressure we feel from the world. Heavenly Father will strengthen us as he did his apostles.

We each may want to look at ourselves carefully and really consider what is important to us in our lives right now. We make decisions based upon what is important to us. If we are choosing the world instead of standing firm for truth and righteousness, then we need to examine our priorities. Heavenly Father can help us make changes in our priorities when necessary, but our desire to change must be greater than our desire to stay the same. Is what is most important to us what really matters the most?

President Ezra Taft Benson asked the young women of the Church for a "renewed commitment to set aside the things of this world. We call upon you to unite in strength and power as you commit to stand for . . . truth and righteousness." Young women have also been reminded that it is their duty to "set examples for others instead of seeking to pattern after them." ("Young Women Worldwide Celebration: 'Stand for Truth and Righteousness,'" November 18, 1989, instructions sent to priesthood and Young Women leaders.)

Remember that the world's way is not the way to peace and happiness. We cannot find peace by following the world. It comes as a result of knowing who we are and standing firm in those things that are most important in life. May we walk tall as we stand for truth and righteousness, showing others that there is a better way than following the world.

CHAPTER ELEVEN

Give a Piece of Your Heart

I had graduated from college and was living at home with my family. The Lawsons, a young family with small children, had moved into a home around the corner from us. We didn't have any small children in our home; my youngest sister was a young teenager. But we still became close friends with this sweet family. I especially became attached to the fourth Lawson child, Mary Ellice. We called her Leecy.

From the time she was born, Leecy was a special little girl to my family and me. Whenever we wanted to have a child in our home, we would go to the Lawsons' and ask to borrow Leecy. Sometimes we would borrow more than one of the Lawson children, but Leecy was always among those we loved to have in our home. I used to tell Mary Lois (Leecy's mother) that she could give me Leecy or any of her children anytime she would like. When Leecy was three years old, her family moved to a new home about twenty minutes away from us. We still kept in close touch and visited them often.

The first Christmas after the Lawsons moved, my brother and sister and I fixed up a large Christmas boot, filled it with goodies and small gifts for the children, and delivered it to the Lawsons the Sunday before Christmas. The children were pleased with our offering, but they seemed more excited about the gift they were going to bring me on Christmas day.

On Christmas afternoon, we saw the Lawsons' station wagon pull up in front of our house. Jody, Lori, Brian, and Zachary came running up to the house with Mary Lois following. Then came Craig, who was carrying a large box. The box was big enough that it was wrapped in at least three different kinds of wrapping paper, and it was heavy enough that it was bulging quite badly at the bottom.

The children were excited as they came into the house and Craig carefully set the box down on the floor by the Christmas tree. The tag taped to the top of the box read, "To Jamie from the Lawsons." The flaps on the top were only folded over, so the top was not sealed tight. Whatever was in the box was not holding very still. By this time I knew what (who) was in the box, but it was fun, at the coaxing of the other Lawson children, to open the flaps and look inside. There was Leecy Lawson, sitting cross-legged in the box, clutching her new Christmas doll. Her mother prodded her a little and said, "Give it to her, Leecy."

With that, Leecy's little hand reached up out of the box, and she handed me a rolled-up scroll that was decorated in red and green and tied with a Christmas ribbon. I unrolled the scroll and read:

To Jamie,
I know how much you wanted me under-
neath your Christmas tree.
But my family with me could not part,
So I give to you . . . a piece of my heart.
Merry Christmas!
Love, Leecy

Mary Lois prompted again and said, "Okay, you can give it to her, Leecy." Leecy's other hand let go of her new Christmas doll and reached out of the box, this time handing me a small package, seemingly wrapped by a three-year-old. Inside the small box was a tiny gold heart charm. Leecy had given to me "a piece of [her] heart." I still wear the charm on a necklace as a wonderful reminder of my favorite Christmas gift.

Perhaps the real gift was the lesson I learned that even though we seldom wrap ourselves up in a box and give ourselves away, we can over and over again bless others' lives by giving a piece of our heart.

Although we can give a piece of our hearts in small and simple ways, the effect and impact on others can be dramatic, even life-changing. We all know how good it feels when our lives are blessed by someone's simple kindness. We may also know the opposite feelings of loneliness, hurt, or the normal need to feel loved. The Golden Rule is not only a good rule to live by; it is also a commandment: "All things whatsoever ye would that men should do to you, do ye even so to them." (Matthew 7:12.) Because it is a commandment, blessings come when we keep it. In some ways it is almost selfish to give because we are blessed by doing so, and it feels so good.

I love the picture I see when I read this scripture: "Give, and it shall be given unto you; good measure, pressed down, and shaken together, and running over, shall men give into your bosom. For with the same measure that ye mete withal it shall be measured to you again." (Luke 6:38.) We receive back more than we give, often simply because we feel good about ourselves and because we feel peace. These are great blessings that come from giving to others.

One day while working a summer job, I left my desk for a few moments. When I returned, a piece of paper was sitting on top of my typewriter. The paper said, "If your name is Jamie, turn this paper over." I qualified, so I turned the paper over and read, "I just want you to know that I appreciate you. Love, Diane." This happened years ago, but I still remember that note and how good it made me feel. It probably took Diane ten seconds to make that effort, but fifteen years later I am still thankful for that simple message and expression.

There is a connection between loving ourselves and loving and serving others. Sister Pat Holland wisely said, "A critical, petty, or vicious remark is simply an attack on our own self-worth. On the other hand, if our minds are constantly seeing good in others, that, too, will return, and we will truly feel good about ourselves" (*On Earth As It Is in Heaven* [Salt Lake City: Deseret Book Co., 1989], p. 29.) How we feel about ourselves is reflected in how we feel about and treat others. And how we feel about and treat others contributes to positive or negative feelings about ourselves. If we feel down on ourselves, chances are we will treat others unkindly. If we treat others unkindly, odds are that we will feel down on ourselves.

The way we treat others reveals a lot about our inner feelings. The ideal is to love ourselves and have good feelings in our hearts. Those feelings will be evident by our outward actions and service to others. Sincere, ongoing love and service come from the heart. Service to others will be short-lived unless our hearts mean it. However, practicing loving and giving to others even if we don't feel it is better than not doing it at all, and it will strengthen our feelings and desire to serve others.

I received a hand-delivered, crayon-created letter from a three-year-old one day—the kind we put on our refrigerator or in our journal. I am not sure what it said, but I know what it meant. The three-year-old giver asked, "Jamie, do you know why I gave you that letter? I gave you the letter because I love you!" "For out of the abundance of the heart the mouth speaketh." (Matthew 12:34.)

We all have days when we focus on major traumas like the new zit on our face, the run in our nylons, or the fact that our new jeans are not the designer label some of our friends wear, and we are sure everyone will notice. Guess what? Seldom does anyone else ever notice those things we are self-conscious about. Why? Because they are so self-conscious and worried about their own little concerns that they think everyone else is noticing. We need to be confident and comfortable enough with ourselves that we can focus outside ourselves and be others-conscious instead of self-conscious.

We can make it our personal challenge to be the one who makes a difference in someone's day and in someone's life. We can choose someone specific, perhaps someone who often goes unnoticed, and do simple things for him or her like saying hello, smiling, or writing a note.

Then we can see if we don't notice a difference developing in that person's attitude and confidence.

It is easy to be kind and giving to those who are kind and giving to us, to those who are our friends. But we need to put ourselves in the place of those who need a friend and who need love—and then befriend them and help them know they are loved. Think about this: "If ye love them which love you, what reward have ye?" (Matthew 5:46.) We are also given this commandment: "Love your enemies, bless them that curse you, do good to them that hate you, and pray for them which despitefully use you, and persecute you." (Matthew 5:44.) That may be difficult, but it is a commandment, and it carries with it blessings. Remember also, "we believe . . . in doing good to *all* men." (Articles of Faith 1:13; emphasis added.)

The question "Who is my neighbour?" was asked of the Savior. He responded by teaching about a man, who, while on his way from Jerusalem to Jericho, fell among thieves, was badly wounded, and was left alone "half dead." (Luke 10:30.) A priest and a Levite both saw the man in need but "passed by on the other side." (V. 31.) It was a Samaritan who had compassion on the injured, and we read that the "the Jews have no dealings with the Samaritans" (John 4:9); they were not the best of friends. The Good Samaritan did not just have a little compassion; instead, he made sure that the injured man was well taken care of. That is "loving our enemies" and "doing good to those that hate us." The Savior's closing words as he taught this parable were, "Go, and do thou likewise." (Luke 10:37.)

Much good would be done if every morning we told

Heavenly Father that we are willing to be an instrument in his hands to bless someone else's life today and asked him to help us to know who might be in need. In speaking of charity, Mormon tells us, "Pray unto the Father with all the energy of heart, that ye may be filled with this love, which he hath bestowed upon all who are true followers of his Son, Jesus Christ." (Moroni 7:48.) When we pray "with all the energy of heart" to be filled with this love, Heavenly Father will not deny us this blessing. We can ask him to bless us to be "rooted and grounded in love." (Ephesians 3:17.) That sounds so firm and solid. We can bless others' lives, and our lives will also be greatly blessed in so doing.

When Holli was a Beehive some years ago, she brought a note card and envelope with her to church one Sunday. She told her Young Women adviser that she had prayed to know who might need a note from her that day, and she felt strongly that there was someone who could use it. Later that day she wrote the note to another girl in the ward, realizing that the girl needed to know she was loved. Haven't we all had experiences when we have really thought about certain people, wondering how they are and feeling concerned for their well-being? When those thoughts come and we feel that way, it may be important for us to take action. We need to follow our feelings, act on those promptings, and in some way let the people know we are thinking about them. Those thoughts and feelings may be coming from Heavenly Father, making us aware of someone who needs something we can give.

We probably have had times when someone has written us a note or called us on the phone just when we needed someone to be there for us. We know how good that feels and recognize that Heavenly Father blesses our lives through others. President Spencer W. Kimball taught, "God does notice us, and he watches over us. But it is usually through another mortal that he meets our needs." (*Teachings of Spencer W. Kimball*, p. 252.)

Sister Burbidge lived in my ward a few years ago. Actually, I lived in her ward. She had been living there a long time before I moved in. Most people who knew her affectionately called her Sister B. Sister B was well known for her delicious chocolate chip cookies, and she was unselfish in sharing them with others. During the Christmas season of 1990, the youth and youth leaders in the ward went to visit Sister B to sing Christmas carols and give her a poinsettia. That year she was ninety-five years old. She pushed her wheelchair around the house as she busily prepared root beer floats for her guests, and of course she served chocolate chip cookies. It was supposed to be the youth service project, but she was doing the serving.

Sister B died of natural causes on March 1, 1991. At the viewing the night before her funeral, her grand-daughters and great-granddaughters greeted those waiting in line with plates of chocolate chip cookies. That is not a typical part of a viewing. But then Sister B was not a typical friend and neighbor. The obituary noting the passing of Sister B mentioned her service in the Church, her family, and other details of her life. The last line read, "In lieu of flowers, send chocolate chip cookies to your neighbors." And many did. There were numerous plates of chocolate chip cookies being delivered throughout the neighborhood in the weeks that followed. I am sure many were made using the well-loved recipe of Sister B.

Sister B made a difference—in a simple way, but she made a difference! Not everyone can make chocolate chip cookies the way Sister B did. But we can each make a difference by giving to others in our own way, being ourselves, and giving what we can give best. I drove by a theater one day where a classic Walt Disney movie was playing. In lights on the billboard I read, "10 Dalmatians." Now "10" is quite different from "101," and I realized what a difference "1" can make.

The greatest joys in our lives will come as we give a piece of our heart to others. We do it in our own way, asking Heavenly Father to guide and bless us to be more aware of others' needing what we can give. We *can* make a difference in others' lives. Our purpose in giving is not to be rewarded, but we know that the Lord will "measure to every man according to the measure which he has measured to his fellow man." (D&C 1:10.) May the measure of our reward be "running over." (Luke 6:38.)

CHAPTER TWELVE

Gratitude—Attitude

I am not sure there is a better feeling in all the world than gratitude. It feels good to recognize blessings in our lives and to be grateful for them. It is not the number of blessings we have that determines how grateful we feel but our attitude and recognition of those blessings. Elder Hartman Rector, Jr., has said, "I have never seen a happy person who was not thankful for what he had." (*Ensign,* July 1973, p. 57.) There is a definite correlation between happiness and gratitude.

When we feel gratitude for a blessing, we are doubly blessed—we have a blessing for which we feel grateful, and we have the blessing of feeling gratitude. Someone shared with me this thought from Channing Pollock: "It is good that we should set aside a day in each year for Thanksgiving, but it would be better if we gave thanks every day. For the absence of thankfulness does not mean that we are merely ungrateful—it means that we are missing the thrill of appreciation and pleasure."

We learn a great lesson about gratitude as we read Luke chapter 17. The Savior entered a certain village, and "there met him ten men that were lepers, which stood afar off." (V. 12.) They stood "afar off" because people with leprosy were sent away and shunned because of the fear of this disease. The ten men asked Jesus for mercy, that he would heal them. Jesus told them to go show themselves unto the priests. Even "as they went, they were cleansed." (V. 14.) All ten of them were healed. Only one of them "turned back, and with a loud voice glorified God, and fell down on his face at his feet, giving him thanks." (Vv. 15–16.) Jesus questioned, "Were there not ten cleansed? but where are the nine?" (V. 17.)

The nine others who were healed really received only half of the blessing. They missed the sweet feeling of gratitude and expressing those feelings to the one who healed them. I am sure they felt happy about being cleansed, but a grateful heart magnifies any joy we feel upon receiving a blessing.

There is always something to be grateful for. During really tough times we may need to look hard, but we will find something. Raelene is one of the most positive people I know. She has had some difficult challenges in her life but is always positive and happy and looking for the many good things that she has. One day she locked her keys in her car. That is always frustrating and never convenient. Even though her schedule was hectic, Raelene was patiently waiting for someone to come and help her. Her cheerful comment was, "Oh well, at least I know my keys are safe!" What an attitude that allowed her to feel gratitude.

President Ezra Taft Benson counseled us, "Think more about what you *do* have than what you *don't* have. Dwell upon the goodnesses of the Lord to you." (*Ensign,*

November 1988, p. 97.) This attitude can be learned even if we don't naturally look on the bright side. We can consciously look for good in what we do have and create a more positive and grateful attitude.

One day I was dwelling upon what I didn't have, and I felt unhappy. A friend of mine suggested that I make a list of two hundred things for which I was grateful. I said, "Two hundred things? I certainly don't have that much to be grateful for!" She encouraged me again, so I began my list. I started by listing separately every member of my family. I listed every little thing I could think of that made me happy. I began to feel better as I added simple things to my list. That was years ago, and I still remember the pure joy I felt as I wrote "Fritos." I like Fritos and had eaten some that day, and as I thought about it I really did feel grateful.

I finished my list of two hundred things for which I was grateful. Close to the two-hundredth thing I listed was, "I am grateful that I made a list." When we take time to count our blessings one by one, the large and the small ones, we can't help but recognize that we have many reasons to be grateful.

The Lord has said, "He who receiveth all things with thankfulness shall be made glorious; and the things of this earth shall be added unto him, even an hundred fold, yea, more." (D&C 78:19.) It is a glorious feeling to receive "all things with thankfulness." The promise is given that when we do so, more will be added for which we can be grateful.

I remember reading this statement by Ralph Waldo Emerson that was taped to the door of my sister's college dorm room: "Never lose an opportunity of seeing anything that is beautiful. For beauty is God's handwriting. Welcome it in every fair face, in every fair sky, in every fair flower, and thank God for it as a cup of blessing." There are many opportunities to see beautiful things. We need to develop an attitude of looking for them and recognizing them. They are there in the simplest, most common things around us. Thank God for them, for they are each "a cup of blessing."

Annie, Jenny, and Elizabeth were riding in the car with their dad on their way home from the hospital. They had just seen their new baby sister for the first time. Five-year-old Jenny turned to seven-year-old Annie and asked, "Annie, is this the happiest day of your life?"

Annie replied, "Yeah."

Jenny gratefully expressed, "Mine too." They were both basking in a blessing and feeling the happiness that true gratitude brings.

I loved playing "the thankful game" with six-year-old Michelle. She let me sleep in her bed for a week while she slept on a mattress on the floor beside me. When we would go to bed at night she wasn't tired enough to go to sleep, so we would take turns saying what we were thankful for. Our comments ranged from "I am thankful Andrew shared his candy with me" to "I am thankful for my pink T-shirt" to "I am thankful that Michelle is letting me sleep in her bed." We were thankful for many people, lots of good food, and many beautiful things in the world. When Michelle finally got tired and was ready to sleep, she would say, "I am thankful for everything in the world. Now we can go to sleep!" And I am thankful for Michelle.

There are many expressions of gratitude that should be directed to Heavenly Father and many that need to be expressed to other people. My father has always been a good example of someone who expresses gratitude to others. His attitude is one of looking for good things people do and then expressing appreciation to them. I am sure many who have known him have received letters and thank-you notes for talks they have given or for their participation in something my dad knew about. We all know how good it feels when we receive a sincere expression of gratitude or a thank-you for something we have done. We can be the ones to express those thank-yous to others and help them enjoy receiving the thanks as we feel the joy that comes from expressing the feelings.

It seems that my nieces and nephews have inherited their grandfather's kind way. I have a drawer full of "Thank you for the slumber party," "You're the best aunt a kid could ever have," "Thank you for the dollar," "I hope you have a happy birthday," and "I love you" notes from them. It is not that what I have done is so great but that they have been taught to recognize grateful and loving feelings and to express them. It means a lot to me to receive such expressions.

If we do not tell people that we appreciate them or are grateful for something they have done, they may never know. They may need to hear it, and we may need just as much to express it. I heard a statement many years ago that I will always remember: "How will they know unless you tell them?" They probably won't, and that is too bad.

There are many reasons we don't express gratitude even when we feel it. Whatever the reasons, I am not sure they are good enough. We read of this command in more than one reference in the scriptures: "In every thing give thanks" (1 Thessalonians 5:18; see also D&C 98:1). When it comes to thanking Heavenly Father, we should not neglect expressing our gratitude to him. Again, the command is clear: "Thou shalt thank the Lord thy God in all things." (D&C 59:7.) President Marion G. Romney, referring to this scripture, said, "It is perfectly evident from this scripture that to thank the Lord in all things is not merely a courtesy, it is a *commandment* as binding upon us as any other commandment." (*Ensign*, November 1982, p. 50.)

I think one of the reasons Heavenly Father wants us to express gratitude to him is because he knows how good we will feel when we recognize and express those feelings. We also read that God is offended when we do not recognize his hand: "In nothing doth man offend God, or against none is his wrath kindled, save those who confess not his hand in all things, and obey not his commandments." (D&C 59:21.) Recognizing the hand of God and our indebtedness to him is not a weakness but a strength. Yes, "it is a good thing to give thanks unto the Lord." (Psalm 92:1.)

Nancy was getting married. I was invited to a bridal shower for her that was being given by another friend in the ward. The occasion began like a normal bridal shower. We played several games and ate refreshments, and her fiancé came to kiss the bows out of Nancy's hair as she opened her presents. After the presents were opened, Nancy sat on the floor with a mass of wrinkled wrapping paper strewn about the floor in front of her. Some of the guests were sitting on the floor around her when suddenly Nancy reached for her eye and exclaimed, "Oh no! My contact lens fell out!"

We have all seen what Christmas morning looks like

as gifts are being opened and before the trash bags are filled. That is what it looked like in front of Nancy. Everyone began carefully looking through each piece of used wrapping paper. It seemed hopeless as each piece of paper was carefully unwadded a second time to be sure the tiny contact lens had not been missed. Finally, Nancy stopped looking and confidently said, "I think we need to have a prayer."

Nancy, already kneeling on the floor, bowed her head, folded her arms, and sincerely and honestly talked with Heavenly Father about what was happening. She told him that she knew he was aware of what had happened and that we needed his help to find the contact lens. She prayed for guidance, and she told him that she knew he could help. Her prayer ended, and shortly thereafter Nancy saw the glimmer of the lens on one of the pieces of wrapping paper lying in front of her.

Then Nancy, still in her kneeling position, confidently declared, "I think we need to thank Heavenly Father." She again bowed her head, folded her arms, and sincerely recognized Heavenly Father's guidance as she thanked him for blessing her to find the contact lens.

Some who were at the shower chuckled because this was not a usual occurrence for such an occasion. However, all who were there were taught some great lessons: Heavenly Father can and will guide us, it is okay to ask him, and "it is a good thing to give thanks unto the Lord" (Psalm 92:1). Often we recognize our need for help, so we ask the Lord to guide and bless us. The blessing is given and then all is well, so we go on our way and neglect to thank him. We are leaving out the opportunity for wonderful feelings and some close communication with Heavenly Father if our gratitude is not expressed. I am grateful for Nancy, for her bridal shower, for her lost contact lens, and for the valuable lessons I learned.

A wise person once said, "We are not as grateful as we *could* be, simply because we don't realize how grateful we *should* be." No matter how much gratitude we express to Heavenly Father, we are still very much indebted to him. King Benjamin gave a marvelous message about our indebtedness to God. He said, "If you should render all the thanks and praise which your whole soul has power to possess" to God, and "if ye should serve him with all your whole souls yet ye would be unprofitable servants." (Mosiah 2:20–21.)

King Benjamin continued, "In the first place, he hath created you, and granted unto you your lives, for which ye are indebted unto him. And secondly, he doth require that ye should do as he hath commanded you; for which if ye do, he doth immediately bless you; and therefore he hath paid you. And ye are still indebted unto him, and are, and will be, forever and ever; therefore, of what have ye to boast?" (Mosiah 2:23–24.) We can see that there is no way we can get ahead of God's goodness to us. His blessings are great, and it is a blessing to feel grateful.

I appreciate this statement by President David O. McKay: "Thankfulness is measured by the number of words; gratitude is measured by the nature of our actions. Thankfulness is the beginning of gratitude; gratitude the completion of thankfulness." (In *Conference Report,* October 1955, p. 4.) I often pray, "Heavenly Father, help me to show to you my love and gratitude by the way that I live." Our actions show the true gratitude that our words can only begin to express.

It is wonderful to have a grateful heart and to recognize the blessings we receive from others and from Heavenly Father. Gratitude is a wonderful feeling! May our hearts be full of gratitude, and may we "live in thanksgiving daily." (Alma 34:38.)

Chapter Thirteen

Be Willing to Receive

There are many blessings in this life that can be ours if we are willing to receive them. We may be thinking, "Of course I am willing to receive blessings—just send them to me!" Being willing in this sense is much more than a verbal expression. Our willingness is shown by our desires, commitment, efforts, actions, and obedience. Being willing is part of the Plan, and the blessings we enjoy are largely dependent upon how willing we are to receive them.

In a revelation to Joseph Smith, we are told of spirits being "quickened" and then receiving "a fulness" of the celestial, terrestrial, or telestial glories. (D&C 88:22–31.) We read, "They who remain shall also be quickened; nevertheless, they shall return again to their own place, to enjoy that which they are willing to receive, because they were not willing to enjoy that which they might have received." (V. 32.) Clearly we will "enjoy" only that which by our efforts and obedience we are "willing to receive." We mustn't sell ourselves short and settle for less by being unwilling "to enjoy that which [we] might have received."

Of greatest importance in our lives is our willingness to seek Heavenly Father. We have talked about this in previous chapters. May I repeat Paul's desire, "That they should seek the Lord, if they are *willing* to find him, for he is not far from every one of us." (Acts 17:27, JST; emphasis added.) He is not far from us, and our closeness to him depends upon our willingness to find him.

If we each make a firm decision now that we are willing to follow Heavenly Father and walk the path that he has defined, then our course is set, and other decisions we make will keep us on that path. We know that "the way for man is narrow, but it lieth in a straight course before him." (2 Nephi 9:41.) Some may feel that the path is too narrow or restrictive. So they broaden the path themselves, not realizing that by so doing they have left the road completely. They think they are wiser than he who has "marked the path and led the way." ("How Great the Wisdom and the Love, *Hymns*, 1985, no. 195.) His narrow path gives us more freedom than wandering on any winding road we may find on our own. There are no hidden curves on his path to cause us discomfort or confusion, as "it lieth in a straight course."

Elder Thomas S. Monson spoke in a general conference about the importance of choosing the road we each would follow. He told of approaching an entrance to a major freeway in Salt Lake City. At the on-ramp he noticed three hitchhikers, each holding a homemade sign announcing his desired destination. One sign read "Los Angeles" and one read "Boise." These were common signs to see at this location, as that entrance to the freeway led to either city. The third sign surprised Elder Monson. It read simply, "Anywhere." (*Ensign*, November 1976, p. 51.)

The lost, "take me anywhere" attitude and feelings of this hitchhiker are hard to imagine. He was willing to let someone else, anyone else, decide for him which road he would take. When we know that Heavenly Father and his Plan are real, the road to anywhere will not do for us. We are blessed to know that there is a well-defined path for us to follow, constructed by one who knows all about the journey and the destination. We need to be willing to find and follow that path.

I know we do not keep commandments just becuase by doing so we receive blessings. We keep commandments because we love Heavenly Father and want to obey him. But there is a direct correlation between keeping the commandments and receiving the blessings, and it is on this that I want to focus.

As we search the scriptures, we find numerous statements of what I call the promises of God. These are statements that counsel us to do something and then tell of a blessing we will receive if we follow his counsel. These promises are many, and the blessings are wonderful. Their receipt is dependent upon our being willing and deserving to receive them. As I read these scriptures, I sometimes insert the words "he promises" or "I promise" before I read what the Lord will do as a result of my obedience. May I share just a few of these?

> *Learn of me, and listen to my words; walk in the meekness of my Spirit, and [I promise] you shall have peace in me. (D&C 19:23.)*

> *Trust in the Lord with all thine heart; and lean not unto thine own understanding. In all thy ways acknowl-*

edge him, and [he promises] he shall direct thy paths. (Proverbs 3:5–6.)

Counsel with the Lord in all thy doings, and [he promises] he will direct thee for good. (Alma 37:37.)

If ye will turn to the Lord with full purpose of heart, and put your trust in him, and serve him with all diligence of mind, if ye do this, [he promises] he will, according to his own will and pleasure, deliver you out of bondage. (Mosiah 7:33.)

Blessed are all they who do hunger and thirst after righteousness, for [he promises] they shall be filled with the Holy Ghost. (3 Nephi 12:6.)

[I promise] that he who doeth the works of righteousness shall receive his reward, even peace in this world, and eternal life in the world to come. (D&C 59:23.)

As we read these and the many other promises of God, I wonder why we are not always valiant in fulfilling our part. Wouldn't we love to have peace in him? Then why do we sometimes not learn of him and listen to his words and walk in the meekness of his Spirit? Wouldn't we love to be filled with the Holy Ghost? Of course we would. So do we just half-heartedly think about trying to live righteously, or do we really "hunger and thirst after righteousness," thus qualifying for the promised blessing?

"I, the Lord, am bound when ye do what I say; but when ye do not what I say, ye have no promise." (D&C 82:10.) He is completely trustworthy and will always fulfill his promises, his only limitation being our willingness and effort (or lack of willingness and effort) to do what he asks of us. We need to keep in mind that all he asks us to do will benefit us. He does not give commandments for his own benefit, except that he feels great joy when he can bless his children, and it is his "work and [his] glory—to bring to pass the immortality and eternal life of man." (Moses 1:39.)

The things he has promised us are all that we need to be happy in this life and to be able to return to him. Are we willing to receive them? They include the ultimate promise: "This is the promise that he hath promised us, even eternal life." (1 John 2:25.)

Let's look at a promise of God that has been given to young women through a latter-day prophet. President Ezra Taft Benson promised: "Young women, [I promise] the Book of Mormon will change your life. [I promise] it will fortify you against the evils of our day. [I promise] it will bring a spirituality into your life that no other book will. [I promise] it will be the most important book you will read in preparation for life's challenges. A young woman who knows and loves the Book of Mormon, who has read it several times, who has an abiding testimony of its truthfulness, and who applies its teaching [I promise] will be able to stand against the wiles of the devil and will be a mighty tool in the hands of the Lord." (*Ensign,* November 1986, p. 82.) These are wonderful words and powerful promises. We need these blessings in our lives. Are we willing to do our part?

One summer I was serving in my ward Young Women program and attended youth conference with my girls. One evening after a fun activity, another leader and I were goofing around as we walked back to the dorm. We thought we would arrive there before our girls, because surely they would be goofing around as well. As we walked into our apartment in the dorm, we were laughing and joking around. Then we heard the girls in the living room talking quietly with each other. As we listened for a moment, we could tell that they were reading their favorite scriptures to each other. My friend and I looked at each other, got our scriptures, and joined in that wonderful conversation. I am grateful that those girls believed the promise of a prophet and of the Lord. Each girl was willing to do her part in following their counsel and enjoying it greatly. And these girls were a blessing and an example to their leaders as well.

We can also believe the promise in 2 Nephi 32:3, which says, "Feast upon the words of Christ; for behold, [I promise] the words of Christ will tell you all things what ye should do." Wouldn't we like to be told "all things what [we] should do?" The promise is sure. What another wonderful blessing if we are willing to do our part!

Alma taught of our baptismal covenants, which include being "willing to bear one another's burdens, . . . willing to mourn with those that mourn; . . . comfort those that stand in need of comfort, and to stand as witnesses of God at all times and in all things, and in all places." (Mosiah 18:8–9.) As Young Women, we know well the commitment "to stand as witnesses of God at all times and in all things, and in all places." The promise of God for keeping these covenants is that we may be "redeemed of God, and be numbered with those of the first resurrection, that [we] may have eternal life." (Mosiah 18:9.)

We renew our baptismal covenants as we partake of the sacrament and recommit that we "are willing to take upon [us] the name of [the] Son, and always remember him, and keep his commandments which he hath given [us]." Then we have the wonderful promise "that [we] may always have his Spirit to be with [us]." (Moroni 4:3.) We have made a covenant that we are willing to do these things. Covenants are serious and important, and the blessings that are promised are worth every effort on our part.

At this time in our lives, enduring to the end may not sound all that necessary to us. But the promises of God for doing so are great. They include, "The same shall be saved" (3 Nephi 27:6), "Ye will in nowise be cast out" (Mormon 9:29), "The same shall overcome" (D&C 63:20), and even "You shall have eternal life" (D&C 14:7). Another way of saying "endure to the end" may be to say, "Hang in there." That may sound more applicable to us right now. Sometimes we need to be willing to hang in there, just keep doing our best, and not give up.

Don and Jolene had three small children. Michelle was nine months old, Jared was two and a half, and Jeff was four. One day Jolene and the children were going to run some errands. They all went into the garage. Jolene had buckled Michelle into her car seat and then remembered something she had left inside the house. The boys waited in the garage as Jolene hurried into the house, pushing the automatic garage door opener as she went. About thirty seconds later she returned to see Jared hanging by his hands from the ceiling. He had grabbed onto the bottom of the garage door as it opened, held on tight, and gone clear to the top.

His large brown eyes were wide with fear as he clung to the edge of the heavy door, looking anxiously down at the cement floor eight feet below. Jeff was standing right below Jared, reaching up as high as he could reach, with one hand set below each of Jared's dangling, cowboy-booted feet. Jolene rushed to lift Jared down from this dangerous predicament. In her relief and in realizing how funny it looked to see him hanging from the ceiling, Jolene began to laugh. Jeff, who had watched his little brother rise to the ceiling, didn't see the humor and kept saying, "Mommy, it isn't funny." This is a great story to tell only because it ended well. Way to "hang in there," Jared!

When life calls for us to endure and hang in there, we need to be willing to tighten our grip, pray for strength, and know that someone is always reaching out to us, desiring to soften our fall and support us in our efforts. Jesus Christ is our "big brother" who has endured all things and knows well the difficulties of hanging on. He understands of our needs and situation, and his arms and heart are always there for us.

Let's look at one more promise from a prophet of the Lord. President Ezra Taft Benson stated, "Yes, give me a young woman who loves home and family, who reads and ponders the scriptures daily, who has a burning testimony of the Book of Mormon. Give me a young woman who faithfully attends her church meetings, who is a seminary graduate, who has earned her Young Womanhood Recognition Award and wears it with pride! Give me a young woman who is virtuous and who has maintained her personal purity, who will not settle for less than a temple marriage, and [I promise] I will give you a young woman who will perform miracles for the Lord now and throughout eternity." (*Ensign,* November 1986, p. 84.) Are we willing to do those things required to "perform miracles for the Lord?" What a promise! And it is available to each of us.

I heard of a wise priesthood leader who told the youth in his ward, "If you always do what you've always done, you'll always get what you've always got." We don't need to settle for where we have always been just because we have always been there. We can be willing to do and receive more.

Leonardo da Vinci expressed an honest plea as he prayed, "O Lord, thou givest us everything at the price of an effort." (Quoted by Lloyd D. Newell, "Music and the Spoken Word," March 29, 1992.) "Everything" is ultimately what he would give to us. Each effort we make produces progression that will lead us back to our Father in Heaven to enjoy the greatest of all blessings. May we be willing to receive all of those blessings Heavenly Father has promised and is so willing to give to us.

CHAPTER FOURTEEN

Because of Jesus Christ

*I*t was a few weeks before Christmas. I sat on the floor in my living room with the lights off and Christmas music playing in the background, looking at the scrawny, sparsely boughed Christmas tree I had just decorated. As my roommate and I had looked through the Christmas tree lot earlier that day, we noticed the tree and felt sorry for it, and so we bought it. I remember Julie saying, "Jamie, if we don't buy this tree, no one will." The thought warmed our hearts, and we grew attached to our tree and even named it while we were still there on the Christmas tree lot. We named it Cliff.

The lights on the tree were on, and the decorations sparkled, reflecting the lights as they blinked on and off. As I looked at Cliff, I felt the Christmas peace that somehow comes with the season, and I wondered how this funny-looking tree could make me feel this way. I thought of shopping earlier in the day, with the crowded malls, the long lines, and the full parking lots, and I wondered how I could enjoy it so much. I remembered driving on the snowy, slippery roads, in the busier-than-usual traffic,

113

and I realized I didn't even mind that hazard this time of year.

As I thought about these things and wondered why we feel such special feelings at Christmastime, the thought came clearly—it is because of Jesus Christ. It is because he came into the world that we even have a Christmastime. It is because of him that a tree named Cliff can look so beautiful, and that traffic and lines and snowy roads are okay. It is true that we feel good when we are giving to others, and that is part of Christmas, but we are giving to others because of Jesus. Even people who don't know who he really is and people who don't feel love for him participate in the season and can't help but enjoy its magical influence. Many do not have any idea that they feel the way they feel because of him, but whether they know it or not, it is because of Jesus.

We have talked about the Plan and the great blessing we have of knowing that we have lived with Heavenly Father, that he knows us now, and that we will return to him. A key part of this plan is that we have a Savior, without whom the Plan would not be possible. A marvelous statement is used to define faith as the first of the seven Young Women Values: "I am a daughter of a Heavenly Father who loves me, and I will have faith in his eternal plan, *which centers in Jesus Christ, my Savior.*" (Young Women Values; emphasis added.) Because of him the Plan works, and because of him we can progress in this life and return to Heavenly Father.

There are many important teachings of the gospel and many great things that have taken place in this world. Alma puts things in perspective: "There be many things to come; and behold, there is one thing which is of more importance than they all—for behold, the time is not far distant that the Redeemer liveth and cometh among his people." (Alma 7:7.) Since this is "of more importance than they all," I want to repeat something written in a previous chapter.

Part of what the Savior did for us was to "take upon him death, that he may loose the bands of death which bind his people; and he will take upon him their infirmities, that his bowels may be filled with mercy, according to the flesh, that he may know according to the flesh how to succor his people according to their infirmities." (Alma 7:12.) Because of Jesus Christ, we will live beyond death and can be with Heavenly Father again. We can also know that someone knows and understands all that we go through in our lives. This is part of the Atonement, that he can understand and "succor" us. But we need to recognize him and the fact that he has that power and perspective to bless us. He understands us in a personal, perfect way.

Because of Jesus Christ, we can repent. He can "blot out [our] transgressions." (Alma 7:13.) We all need that blessing. "He suffered the pain of all men, that all men might repent and come unto him." (D&C 18:11.) Without the possibility of repentance, we would be "in a lost and in a fallen state." (1 Nephi 10:6.)

Because of him we can be resurrected. "He cometh into the world that he may save all men if they will hearken unto his voice; . . . and he suffereth this that the resurrection might pass upon all men." (2 Nephi 9:21–22.) He is the one who can save us as we hearken unto his voice. Now, we may not be all that concerned today about being resurrected, but there is more to life than just this very day. The important things that he has done for us are "of more importance than they all." (Alma 7:7.)

I learned one evening that I cannot get through life alone, that I need someone to step in and do for me those things I cannot do for myself. I was driving home one evening from an appointment about twenty miles away. It was dark as I drove north on a major freeway. I was eager to get home and was thinking about the things I needed to be doing, when suddenly my car started to slow down. I was pushing hard on the accelerator, but it did no good. The car was moving slower and slower, just coasting on the flat freeway. I pulled over to the right shoulder of the road, coasting as far as I could, with my car coming to a stop at the top of a freeway off-ramp.

I tried to start the car, but the engine wouldn't quite turn over. I made sure the doors were locked and tried to start it again several times. I had had a prayer in my heart even as the car started to slow down on the freeway, but now I started to pray out loud. First I asked Heavenly Father to protect me. I was nervous. I was all alone and it was dark and I knew nothing about cars. I also asked him to help me know if I should do anything besides just sit in the car and wait for someone to come and help me. The freeway was crowded and this was a busy off-ramp, but I felt very much alone as cars sped by and no one seemed to notice my car, with its emergency lights flashing, parked on the side of the road. If I did leave my car, I didn't know if I would find a telephone close by or if I would be wandering in the dark searching for one. I felt very uncomfortable.

Fifteen or twenty minutes went by, and then in the shadows I could see someone walking up the side of the off-ramp. I kept praying for protection and wisdom. I could see the figure of a man wearing a hooded sweat-shirt getting closer as he walked quickly along the side of the road. I became more nervous as I sat in the car pretending I wasn't there. I don't know if he saw me or not, but he walked past my car and continued walking on the side of the road. I expressed gratitude for my safety, and my conversation with Heavenly Father continued. I kept telling him that I was nervous and that I knew I needed someone to help me. Clearly I would need someone to step into this situation, maybe a highway patrolman, the driver of a tow truck, someone to pick me up and take me to a telephone, or someone to drive me to my home. I could not do this by myself.

I had been sitting in my car on the side of the road for nearly an hour when the feeling came that I should leave the car. I quickly gathered my keys and my purse, got out of the car, locked the door, and started running on the side of the road down the off-ramp. The first vehicle to pass me was a truck. As it passed, I saw the brake lights come on. Then it pulled over to the side of the road, and the back-up lights brightened as the truck moved back and stopped in front of me. A woman unrolled the window and said, "It looks like you need some help." I climbed into the cab of the truck as this kind family drove me to the nearest telephone, more than a mile away. I called a towing company to come get my car and then called a friend to pick me up and take me home.

Even as I sat in the dark alone, I was thinking about a bigger picture. I realized that at times we need someone to come to our aid and bridge the gaps that we cannot bridge for ourselves. There are times when we have gone to our limit and have done all that we can do but more needs to be done. Someone else needs to step in and do what we cannot do for ourselves. Through the Atonement, Jesus Christ is the one who can bridge the gaps in our lives and do those things we cannot do for ourselves. He bridges the gap between life and death, making eternal life possible for us. More immediately, he bridges gaps in our lives with forgiveness, with healing, with increased patience, with strength when our strength seems to be gone, with knowledge beyond our own learning, with new understanding, and with peace that only he can give. We cannot make it in life alone. We cannot make it without him.

The counsel of Helaman to his sons Nephi and Lehi is powerful counsel for us: "Remember, remember that it is upon the rock of our Redeemer, who is Christ, the Son of God, that ye must build your foundation; that when the devil shall send forth his mighty winds, yea, his shafts in the whirlwind, yea, when all his hail and his mighty storm shall beat upon you, it shall have no power over you to drag you down to the gulf of misery and endless wo, because of the rock upon which ye are built, which is a sure foundation, a foundation whereon if men build they cannot fall." (Helaman 5:12.) Jesus Christ is the sure foundation upon which our lives must be built.

I cannot comprehend all that the Savior has done for us. I am grateful that "the principal question before us is not do we comprehend the Atonement, but do we accept it?" (George Q. Morris, in *Conference Report*, April 1956, p. 112.) I do accept the Atonement. What I do understand about what the Savior has done for us, I love, and what I do not yet understand, I trust. Speaking of the Savior and the Atonement, Elder Joseph B. Wirthlin has said, "Who he is and what he does affected each of us before we were born and will affect us each day of our mortal lives and throughout the eternities. . . . The Atonement . . . is an act of love for which we should be more grateful than for any other blessing or gift of God." (*Ensign*, November 1993, pp. 5–6.)

My brother and sister-in-law and their five children moved to Hawaii one July. All the children had adjusted well and made new friends except four-year-old Andrew, who was struggling without a good friend and wanted to go home to where they used to live. His parents often expressed to extended family members their concern for Andrew, and we were all praying that he would find a good friend and be happy. He has the greatest smile in the world, and it hurt my heart to think of his being unhappy.

One morning late in November, Andrew got out of bed and sought out his mother in another room. Andrew looked happier than she had seem him in several months. He said to her, "Mommy, I wish you and Daddy could see what Jesus really looks like too." Then he told her about his dream. He explained that in the dream he and his brothers and sister were jumping on the bed when they looked out the window and saw Jesus coming down past the window and standing on the lawn. They ran outside to see him better. Andrew said, "None of us were scared when we saw him. Even Timmy wasn't scared." (Timmy is Andrew's little brother.) Andrew said that Jesus was wearing white clothes and had a brown beard. Then, with real joy behind his sweet voice, he told his mother, "It made me feel so good inside."

Andrew called me on the telephone later that morning to tell me about his dream. I told him I wished I could have seen his dream. I asked him if Jesus was kind. He said, "Oh, yes." I asked him if he knew that Jesus loves him, and he said, "Oh, yes!" I know he really felt that love. That was a very real experience for Andrew and has made a difference in his life. I know Heavenly Father knew that this dear little boy needed to feel something special. It was because of Jesus Christ and the blessing of feeling of his love that Andrew was able to "feel so good inside."

I know that the Savior's love is real and that he gave his life for each of us. I want to learn more about him and become more like him. The good things in life come because of him: "In Christ there should come every good thing." (Moroni 7:22.) He is the giver of all good gifts and has given us many. We should rejoice in all of those many good gifts and "in him who is the giver of the gift." (D&C 88:33.)

May we know that we do not have to live our lives without him. May we be blessed with comfort and peace from him. May the gaps in our lives be bridged by him. May we "always remember him, and . . . always have his Spirit to be with [us]." (Moroni 4:3.) May we know that what he has done for us "is of more importance than they all" (Alma 7:7) and build our foundation surely and firmly upon him. May we, like Andrew, "feel so good inside" as we feel his personal love for us. And may we be blessed with every good thing, remembering always the Source of all that is good—yes, it is Jesus Christ.

Index